Marriage Equality:

Why Same-sex Marriage Is Good for the Church and Nation

Rev. Steven F. Kindle

Second Revised Edition

EnerPower Press
Gonzalez, Florida
2017

Unless otherwise indicated, all Scripture quotations are from the New
Revised Standard Version Bible, copyright © 1989 by the Division of
Christian Education of the National Council of the Churches of Christ
in the U. S. A. Used by permission. All rights reserved.

From Trinity Stores website:
"Sts. Sergius and Bacchus are ancient Christian martyrs who were
tortured to death in Syria because they refused to attend sacrifices in
honor of Jupiter. Recent attention to early Greek manuscripts has also
revealed that they were openly gay men and that they were erastai or
lovers. These manuscripts are found in various libraries in Europe and
indicate an earlier Christian acceptance of homosexuality."

ISBN10: 1-63199-399-2
ISBN13: 978-1-63199-399-2
Library of Congress Control Number: 2017943424

EnerPower Press
P. O. Box 841
Gonzalez, FL 32560

energion.com
pubs@energion.com

(EnerPower Press is an imprint of Energion Publications)

DEDICATION

To Diane,
partner in life and ministry
whose sacrifices and unwavering support
made this book possible

and to our

Allies in the struggle

ACKNOWLEDGEMENTS

My thanks to the Rev. Dr. Mel White, co-founder of Soulforce and an early encourager of my ministry with Clergy United. His influence and example of Christian integrity permeate this book.

The Reverend Doctor Robert Cornwall, pastor, writer, editor and friend, looked over the manuscript and offered the advice of a seasoned and artful eye. Should this book evidence any shortcomings, it's because I failed to follow his lead.

A special acknowledgement goes to the many people who sat through my seminars over the years. Your penetrating questions and authentic need for answers kept me moving forward with my research.

To my friends in the gay community, you constantly inspire me. I hope this book will serve to make your life better in exchange for how you have enriched mine.

And to Niles Discovery Church of Fremont, California and their pastor, Jeff Spencer: For your modeling of a congregation fully utilizing the gifts of gay and straight Christians alike, I owe a debt of gratitude and remain in awe of your transforming grace.

The chapter, Word to Pastors, is from my article, "When Welcoming Is More Than Toleration," first published in the AP Clergy Journal, with permission of the Academy of Parish Clergy.

The picture on the cover is ©"Sergious and Bacchus," by Brother Robert Lentz, O.F.M. Courtesy of Trinity Stores, www.trinitystores.com, 800.699.4482

TABLE OF CONTENTS

Foreword

Since you are reading this book you are serious about engaging the specific issues surrounding same-sex marriage and Lesbians, Gays, Bisexuals and Transgenders (LGBTs) in general. What you are about to read is intended to give you a well-rounded introduction to the many aspects of gay Americans and the need for comprehensive gay rights, especially the rights that all married heterosexual couples enjoy and are currently withheld from same-sex couples.

This book comes from the hand of a straight ally who has been part of the Gay Rights movement for over twenty years. I am also an ordained minister who has studied these issues both from first-hand observation and academic research. I will be the first to admit that I am not a scholar. You should find that reassuring, for I don't pretend to present anything that isn't already a consensus in scientific and scholarly circles. I see myself as a midwife who delivers to you the best information available.

I did my primary research in the San Francisco Bay area, where three first-class seminary libraries are available to me, as well as the University of California, Berkeley libraries, a luxury most readers likely won't have. Therefore, whenever possible, I chose to cite references that anyone can follow on the internet. I cite only reputable sources, and a more comprehensive, annotated bibliography is included, as well. You will be introduced to the scholarly works, mostly in footnotes, should you wish to delve deeper into the subjects.

A word about vocabulary: I will use LGBT, nonheterosexual, and gay interchangeably. In most cases, they are comprehensive for the community as a whole. There is a listing of all the terms and definitions used later in the book. I also hold to the convention of inclusive language, even though it sometimes creates awkward sentences. So bear with me in this venture; worlds are created through speech and the world of this book supports equality for all.

All Bible verses are from the New Revised Standard Version (NRSV) unless stated otherwise.

If you are a Christian, you may be exposed for the first time to ideas and conclusions that go against what you have been taught. That, too, is good. Unexamined assumptions aren't really owned by us, yet they rule us night and day. If we're not challenged, we will never escape our self-imprisonment.

If you are not a Christian, you will find much in here that transcends religion and will be useful to you. Many of the conversations you have and the positions taken often center around conservative Christian interpretations. You may find these conversations unsettling, even annoying, and they often lead nowhere. This book will help you understand this mindset so that you can follow their arguments more closely. You might even hazard a rejoinder from time to time. So to all I say, welcome and peace.

You will notice a small amount of repetition. This book is meant to be read mostly in its entirety. However, some of the chapters will be separated out by readers interested in only a few of the topics. In order to be as clear as possible, some duplication of previous material is necessary.

At the time of publication, June of 2013, the United States Supreme Court (SCOTUS) had not ruled on California's Proposition 8 or the Defense of Marriage Act (DOMA). Nevertheless, the substance of this book will not be affected by any ruling that is made. In chapter 9, the possible decisions, are outlined. The affect the decisions have on America and the gay community are anticipated, so the reader will only need to consult the relevant rulings and ignore the others.

Should you wish to correspond with me, I can be reached at info@clergyunited.org. I will attempt to answer any serious inquiry you may have.

Preface to the Second Edition

As recently as 2001, Americans opposed same-sex marriage by a 57% to 35% margin, according to Pew Research and other polling. Since then, support for same-sex marriage has steadily grown. Based on polling in 2015, a majority of Americans now support same-sex marriage, currently about 60%, compared to 39% in opposition. That's a stark reversal in such a very short time. This book is an explanation for this dramatic turnaround in public opinion.

When this book was first published in 2013, America was still awaiting the US Supreme Court rulings on California's Proposition 8 or the Defense of Marriage Act (DOMA). On these two cases would depend the immediate and possibly long-term future of LGBTs in America.

June 26, 2013, turned out to be a most decisive day. On this day, the Supreme Court found Section 3 of DOMA to be unconstitutional, "as a deprivation of the liberty of the person protected by the Fifth Amendment." It also ruled that Prop 8 petitioners had no standing and allowed same-sex marriages to resume in California. After a few months of sorting out the legal and procedural details of both SCOTUS decisions, same-sex marriages are now legal in all 50 states.

Supporters of marriage equality would be tempted to sit back and relax, feeling the struggle is over and won. However, this is far from reality. True, the majority of Americans are now supportive, and the initial challenges to the law have been overturned. Yet, there are significant political voices that are calling for a revamping of the Supreme Court by appointing justices favorable to overturning marriage equality. Nearly every Republican presidential candidate is on record to end it. The presidential election year of 2016 could make a potential reversal a reality.

Mel White, co-founder of Soulforce, and author of the ground-breaking, *Stranger at the Gate*, says the book you are holding is "a veritable library of important resources." If we are to continue to hold back the relentless onslaught to overturn the important and necessary gains we have made to continue the right of all Americans to marriage equality, the information in this book is essential to the task. Here are some of the reasons why:

- The most significant reason that minds are changed is that we have come to know many gays and lesbians. Chapter 1 introduces us to many of them, and we see how utterly normal they are; in fact, they are just like the rest of Americans.

- So much has been written and preached about the so-called "gay agenda," that people are confused about what it is. Chapter 2 deals with what it is and why we continue to need it.

- Chapter 3 shows the horrifying results of keeping gays and lesbians in "the closet." Because many families continue to ostracize their gay children, many still live hidden away. We still need to create space for LGBTs so they can live normal lives, lives lived true to themselves.

- "Traditional marriage" is anything but traditional. It is a yearning for an ideal that never was. Chapter 4 traces the evolving notions of marriage from biblical times to our day to focus on how marriage changes as civilizations evolve. To keep marriage equality for the future requires understanding this.

- Now that the debris of false information has been swept from the floor, we can now look at the issue of gay marriage without needless distraction. That's what we do in Chapter 5. Enough time has passed (seven decades of gay couples have been studied) for us to begin to measure the results. Not surprisingly, gay couples and straight couples come out even.

- One of the most important reasons why Americans change their minds and become supportive of marriage equality is that we are realizing that sexual orientation is not a choice. Chapter 6 surveys the psychological community and its findings that support how we are born with our sexuality intact. It also debunks many of the false claims about homosexuality.

- Most conservative Christians remain committed to a literal understanding of the Bible that seems to condemn LGBTs. They are unlikely to change their minds, but there are many open-minded people who will listen to more recent scholarship showing how this is a misinterpretation of the Bible. Chapter 7 offers a comprehensive look at the data.

- Little has been said about the rich community of LGBTs and what they can offer America given the opportunity to live their lives with the same freedom as everyone else. Chapter 8 looks at the witness of gayness and how it enhances life in our churches, synagogues, and the wider community.

I don't believe it's time to relax and enjoy our hard-won victories. We are in a period where all this could easily slip away. The information in this book can be a helpful bulwark against the possible erosion and eventual elimination of marriage equality and gay acceptance in general. Too many of our gay friends and family members have suffered for us to abandon them now.

As a straight ally in the struggle for gay rights, I offer this book to gay and straight alike with the hope that works such as this will become unnecessary in the not too distant future. Just as Millennials today can't imagine a time when black Americans were oppressed by segregation laws, so may the day soon come when being gay is no longer controversial, but fully appreciated by the human community. —Ash Wednesday, 2016

INTRODUCTION

Homophobia is the last respectable bigotry in America
~ Byrne Fone

Gays in America (and elsewhere) live under an oppressive double standard: They are expected to comport themselves with the same propriety as everyone else, yet they are not given the governmental and societal support undergirding everyone else. This playing field needs to be leveled.

Edith "Edie" Windsor and Thea Spyer, residents of New York, married in 2007. They were together 47 years as a couple. Spyer died in 2009, and because of the Federal Defense of Marriage Act (DOMA) which recognizes only unions between a male and a female, Windsor was required to pay more than $363,000 in federal estate taxes on her inheritance of her wife's estate. If federal law treated her marriage equally with opposite-sex couples' marriages, she would have paid nothing. Her challenge to DOMA became *United States v. Windsor* before the Supreme Court.

Janice Langbehn and Lisa Pond, partners for 18 years, were on a vacation in Florida when Lisa suffered an aneurysm and died in a local hospital. Janice's attempt to visit her dying loved one was repeatedly blocked because she wasn't considered a family member, even though they had adopted and raised children together.

In the United States today, many thousands of same-sex couples who are legally married are denied spousal Social Security benefits because the Federal Government does not acknowledge their marriage. This is only one of an estimated 1,139 benefits, rights and protections provided on the basis of marital status in federal law.

Due to the lack of federal law, in 29 states lesbians, gays, bisexuals, and transgender citizens can be barred from housing, jobs, and even private institutions such as the Boy Scouts of America. Even the suspicion that someone is gay is enough. In many Christian churches and denominations, LGBTs are restricted to attending services only, and cannot participate in preaching, teaching, governing, and are often denied communion. And this treatment is from an institution that is supposed to acknowledge the inherent value of every human being.

If we were observing this degree of discrimination against blacks, or Jews, or the disabled, we would be outraged. But we're not. This book is an effort to bring to light the many misrepresentations and outright lies that currently circulate about the gay community, and to replace them with facts.

Recent polling makes it clear that the opposition to same-sex marriage is based upon unfamiliarity with just who these LGBT people are. As long as we don't know them personally, they remain vague, shadowy figures, subject to all the false stereotypes attributed to them. However, the past experience of the last few decades is changing all this. As the Gay Rights movement gained momentum, more and more LGBTs emerged from the closet. We now know them as our sons and daughters, nieces and nephews, co-workers, neighbors, pastors, friends, and even our moms and dads. This has made all the difference.

It is my contention, and I hope to demonstrate this in the following pages, that our gay population is as normal as the rest of us. That they represent no threat to our society in any way, and that includes to traditional marriage. In fact, granting equal rights—across the board—will only strengthen the fabric of America.

I am writing as a recovering homophobe. My journey began where most Americans my age begin, with all the notions that our culture bestows upon us, including a deep conviction that homosexuals are somehow so different from "normal" people that they shouldn't be included in polite society, that their nature is aggressively sexual, that our children are unsafe around them, that they are psychologically deviant, that they choose their "lifestyle," and they are deserving of hell. What you will see in the remainder of this book is how I discovered how wrong I was.

Why would a straight, married Christian pastor, with no gay children, want to get mixed up in such a controversial, hate-filled and possibly career-ending ministry in support of LGBTs? Especially when there's absolutely no pressure on me to do so. No, I don't have a death wish, or have a gay lover secreted away somewhere. I'm basically a normal guy. I shy away from confrontation and go out of my way to find mutually satisfying outcomes in disputes.

So, what am I doing here? Very simply, I've learned that the gospel of Jesus Christ compels me to come to the side of the oppressed wherever and whenever they're found. Harvard's Byrne Fone calls homophobia "the last respectable bigotry in America." Christians may not be responsible for creating homophobia, but we sure are responsible for helping to maintaining it. Victims of spiritual abuse (not to mention, for now, physical abuse) abound. They have literally been driven from the churches. They have been demonized, scapegoated and condemned for so long and so often that to find one out of the closet in a congregation beats the odds of winning the lottery. We should be ashamed, but we are not; we should repent, but we do not. And the most amazing thing of all is that we need, for our own sake, the presence of nonheterosexual Christians in our congregations and don't have a clue as to why.

I don't come to this struggle as their savior; I come as a grateful ally who has received much from the gay community and have more to learn from them about being a Christian.

This book is mostly about the need for marriage equality. This issue is the pinnacle of accomplishment in welcoming LGBTs fully into America's heart and soul. If this goal is achieved, nothing else really matters. Our gay citizens will finally be considered on equal footing with everyone else. But in order to defend the proposition that LGBTs should be granted the privilege and responsibilities involved with marriage, we first need to clear out some of the underbrush of misunderstandings and outright lies that are awash in our nation concerning nonheterosexual people.

So we will have to establish first that gays are as normal as any random group of Americans; that they are not finally deserving of full inclusion— rather, they have been solid citizens all along. We've just been either too prejudiced or uncaring to notice. We will also delve into the false stereotypes that have driven the discussion to this point. We will look at the history of marriage in the West and discover that marriage is always evolving. We will ask what impact same-sex marriage will have on America, and look at the common objections to it.

We will also take a serious look at the Bible and theology to see what's really behind the mindset of condemnation that permeates many churches. The texts in question seem to support gay exclusion and forbid marriage between people of the same-sex. But that is merely the surface reading and use of texts as pretexts for otherwise held beliefs, as we shall see.

The legal and constitutional issues will also be addressed that weigh on the Supreme Court of the United States with suggestions for where we go from here.

The final chapter offers concrete suggestions for getting involved, and offers ways we can better communicate the message of marriage equality.

This book, then, is an effort to bring the straight church and America to its senses. It is an effort to bring the message of the inclusive gospel that will confront us with our sins and bring us to our knees. It is a plea to those LGBTs we've textually abused not to abandon us, but to nurture us and witness to the life changing power of Jesus.

My conclusions were not reached easily or quickly. I don't expect you to immediately embrace all I've written in this book. I do suspect you will give it serious consideration, as you are now in the process of reading it. That is all I can ask for, a proper hearing. Add to that, prayer for discernment, and if you have not considered this before, seek out Christian gays.

I have presented seminars on the Bible and gay issues all over the country. The same kind of people seemed to show up over and over. The first group is the "moveable middle," those who are truly seeking to find out as much as they can about the issues. Many are parents of gay children, others are pastors of churches or their lay leaders, and still others are there because they would like to see if there is any way a Christian can be supportive of gay inclusion in the church in spite of what they have been taught.

The second group were LGBTs, many of whom left their churches, or I should say were driven out by the spiritual violence so often spewed from the pulpit, and told in so many ways that they aren't welcome. A few were those who remain in spite of the hostility and just needed to be reassured that God still loves them.

A third group was composed of friends and allies of the gay community who are always looking for more information. They all have in common the desire to broaden their understanding and effectiveness. Since you are reading this book, you likely fit into one or more of these categories. So whether you need convincing, reassurance, or information, this book is intended for you.

A Snapshot of Gay Americans

This is our big chance to see what people think of us.
The real us. We have to show 'em
there's nothing to be afraid of.
~ Lisi Harrison, Monster High

It shouldn't be surprising that the 2010 U. S. Census begins its section on "Counting Same-sex Couples" with this caveat: "Official Estimates and Unofficial Guesses."[1] There is no definitive answer to the question of what percentage of the population is nonheterosexual. Kinsey's original reporting of 10% wasn't intended as anything more than a suggestion of how many men experimented with same-sex relationships during their formative years. Even that estimate has been revised over time. Today we are still guessing, but the guesses are getting closer and closer to reality. Why we may not soon get to a reliable number is due to the fact that an unknown percentage of the gay population remains closeted. The most reliable estimates put the figure at about 4%.[2]

The reality is that gays are everywhere and are important contributors to every facet of society. The U.S. Census puts it this way. "Gay and lesbian Americans serve as public servants, scientists, athletes, artists, educators, administrators, statisticians, mathema-

---

1   http://www.census.gov/hhes/samesex/files/counting-paper.pdf
2   http://thenewcivilrightsmovement.com/study-shows-how-many-
     americans-are-gay-lesbian-bisexual-transgender/news/2011/04/07/18551

ticians, researchers, etc., and thus, make significant contributions to the Census Bureau, the Department of Commerce, and this Nation."[1] Yes, gay Americans are everywhere and highly involved with our lives. Even at 4%, this represents a huge slice of our population, now numbering more than 14 million people. Given that American Jews make up only 1½% of the American population, it doesn't take a large population to make a significant impact.

Here's the kicker: the reason most people can name only a few, if any, public servants, scientists, athletes, artists, educators, administrators, statisticians, mathematicians, researchers, etc., is because they are so much like everyone else in our society that they don't stand out as different. They lead lives that are no different from the rest of us, no more or less substantial on the average, and certainly no more or less controversial.

Unfortunately, because the general public has been exposed mostly to sensational media reports, they're left with the impression that all gays are exhibitionist party-animals who only care about their hedonistic lifestyle. It must also be said that this does not fit the vast majority of LGTB people at all. The prejudicial depiction of the stereotypical gay is a product of projecting a minority of Gay Pride parade participants as typical of the whole. Even in a pride parade, the exhibitionists are in the minority.

To say that all gays are like this is to say that all straights are like the party animals participating at the Mardi Gras. A woman in one of my seminars asserted that all gays are promiscuous, "just like in the parades." To which I replied, "So, if I throw a woman a necklace of glass beads, she would flash me, right? That's how straight women behave." She got the point. The fact is that most gays are indistinguishable from straights. The proof is that hundreds of them live in close proximity to many of us and we don't even know it!

The following is a list, by no means exhaustive, of some of the more notable gay Americans. Some will be familiar, others not,

---

1   http://www.census.gov/eeo/special_emphasis_programs/globe_month.
    html

but all of them made important contributions to America. They are drawn from all the categories suggested by the U.S. Census.

Eric Allman is an American computer programmer who developed "sendmail" and its precursor "delivermail" in the late 1970s and early 1980s at UC Berkeley.

James Beard was an American chef and food writer.

Allan Bloom was an American philosopher, classicist, and academic.

Aaron Copland was an American composer, composition teacher, writer, and later in his career a conductor of his own and other American music.

Catherine "Cat" Cora is a professional chef best known for her featured role as an "Iron Chef" on the Food Network television show Iron Chef America.

Barney Frank was the U.S. Representative for Massachusetts's 4th congressional district. A member of the Democratic Party, he is the former chairman of the House Financial Services Committee (2007–2011) and is considered the most prominent gay politician in the United States.

David Geffen is an American record executive, film producer, theatrical producer and philanthropist. Geffen was also one of the three founders of DreamWorks.

Lt. Laurel Hester was a New Jersey police officer who rose to national attention with her deathbed appeal for the extension of pension benefits to domestic partners.

Mychal F. Judge, OFM was a Roman Catholic priest of the Franciscan Order of Friars Minor, Chaplain of the Fire Department of New York and the first certified fatality of the September 11, 2001 attacks.

Bernard King is a retired American professional basketball player. He played fourteen seasons at the small forward position in the NBA.

Rives Kistler is an American attorney and judge in the state of Oregon.

Suze Orman is an American financial advisor, author, motivational speaker, and television host.

Marshall McKusick is a computer scientist, known for his extensive work on BSD, from the 1980s to FreeBSD in the present day.

Richard Pillard is a professor of psychiatry at the Boston University School of Medicine best known for his work on biology and sexual orientation. He was the first openly gay psychiatrist in the United States.

James B. Pollack was an American astrophysicist who worked for NASA's Ames Research Center.

Cole Porter was an American composer and songwriter.

Lionel H. ("Spike") Pries was a leading architect, artist, and educator in the Pacific Northwest.

Thomas Roberts is an American journalist who, since April 2010, serves as a news anchor for MSNBC.

Anthony D. Romero is the American executive director of the American Civil Liberties Union.

Oliver "Billy" Sipple was a decorated U.S. Marine and Vietnam War veteran widely known for saving the life of U.S. President Gerald Ford during an assassination attempt by Sara Jane Moore.

The Very Reverend Robert V. Taylor is a priest in the Episcopal Church USA and an activist for social justice. He was installed in 1999 as dean of St. Mark's Episcopal Cathedral in Seattle, making him the first openly gay Episcopal dean in the United States.

William Thetford was trained as a psychologist and remained professionally active in this field throughout his life. Most associated with co-creating *A Course in Miracles*.

Michael Tilson Thomas is an American conductor, pianist and composer. He is currently music director of the San Francisco Symphony.

Lupe Valdez is an American law enforcement official and the Sheriff of Dallas County, Texas. She is Texas's only elected female sheriff, as well as being the only openly lesbian holder of that office.

Kenji Yoshino is a legal scholar and the Chief Justice Earl Warren Professor of Constitutional Law at New York University School of Law. [1]

This list could be extended indefinitely.[2] You can see that the U.S. Census was right in their observation that gay Americans come from all over the spectrum of contributors to our way of life. It could also have included others like Jeffrey Dahmer, the infamous serial killer, which would only confirm the reality that gays come in all the varieties that make up humanity. There is no need to belabor this point, just as there is no need to make a distinction between straights and gays. We are one and the same. As I say to those who would argue the point, "You don't know enough gays!"

The Kinsey Report and LGBTWIQAs

The first time someone is exposed to the alphabet soup of acronyms used in shorthand for the gay community, it's no wonder there is confusion. It can be bewildering. Often the first question is why there are so many different designations for people's sexual orientations. For that, we must take a quick look at Alfred Kinsey's book, *Sexual Behavior in the Male.* On page 639 we find this seminal conclusion which still holds today:

> Males do not represent two discrete populations, heterosexual and homosexual. The world is not to be divided into sheep and goats. Not all things are black nor all things white. It is a fundamental of taxonomy that nature rarely deals with discrete categories. Only the human mind invents categories and tries to force facts into separated pigeon-holes. The living world is a continuum in each and every one of its aspects. The sooner we learn this concerning human sexual behavior, the sooner we shall reach a sound understanding of the realities of sex.

---

1   These and more can be found here: http://www.ranker.com/list/famous-gay-americans-and-homosexuals-born-in-the-usa/famous-gay-and-lesbian

2   http://en.wikipedia.org/wiki/List_of_gay,_lesbian_or_bisexual_people

Most of us grow up thinking that there is only one kind of sexual orientation—straight. Soon we are introduced to what is presented as a deviant orientation, homosexuality. So, now we know there are two, but one is natural and one is unnatural. Eventually we learn of those who can "swing both ways," and our horizon is stretched to three. Yet Kinsey and those who succeeded him developed and expanded his research to discover that even these classifications are limiting. The following chart illustrates this situation: [Figure 1]

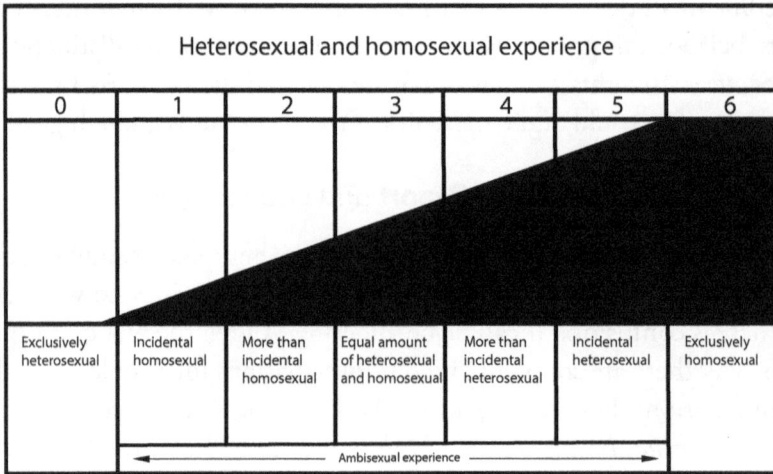

Heterosexual and homosexual experience						
0	1	2	3	4	5	6
Exclusively heterosexual	Incidental homosexual	More than incidental homosexual	Equal amount of heterosexual and homosexual	More than incidental heterosexual	Incidental heterosexual	Exclusively homosexual

◄──────────── Ambisexual experience ────────────►

[Figure 1]

The 0 on the far left represents a heterosexual person with no homosexual tendencies whatsoever. The 6 on the far left represents a homosexual person with no heterosexual tendencies whatsoever. These are the extremes on the chart and in life. Most of us fall somewhere in between. The living world is, indeed, a continuum.

To cloud the issue even further, Wikipedia notes that the

> Kinsey Scale does not address all possible sexual expressions. Others have stepped forward to define it further. In 1980, Michael Storms proposed a two dimensional chart with an X and Y axis. This scale took into account the case of asex-

uality and the simultaneous expression of hetero-eroticism and homo-eroticism. Fritz Klein, in his Sexual Orientation Grid, included factors such as how orientation can change throughout a person's lifetime, as well as emotional and social orientation.

> Kinsey, Storm, and Klein are only three of more than 200 scales to measure and describe sexual orientation. For example there are scales that rate homosexual behaviors from 1 to 14, and measures for gender, masculinity, femininity, transsexualism and attitudes towards contraceptives.[1]

Are you bewildered yet? Heterosexuals have a problem with the notion that sexuality is a continuum because we have been programmed since we were very young to believe that only one way is natural. And that anything other than this is unnatural. Any farm boy or girl can tell you that when it comes to animals, anything goes.

Bruce Bagermihl is a biological research scientist and author. He writes,

> Homosexual behavior occurs in more than 450 kinds of animals worldwide, and is found in every major geographic region and every major animal group. The world is indeed teeming with homosexual, bisexual, and transgendered creatures of every stripe and feather. It is no longer possible to attribute the diversity of human sexual expression solely to the influence of culture or history since such diversity may in fact be part of our biological endowment, an inherent capacity for 'sexual plasticity' that is shared with many other species.[2]

A recent study confirms Bagermihl's work and states that homosexuality in the animal kingdom is virtually universal.[3]

We will return to the natural/unnatural debate when we examine what the Bible says about all this. But for now, we must at

---

1   http://en.wikipedia.org/wiki/Kinsey_scale
2   *Biological Exuberance, Animal Homosexuality and Natural Diversity, p.*
3   *"Same-sex Behavior Seen among All Animals." Physorg.com. 2009-06-16.*

least admit that the scientific evidence for the normality of many sexual orientations is difficult to ignore.

Breaking down the acronym

The use of LGBTQIQA and variants represent a shorthand way of communicating the whole of the gay community. (Recall, I use "gay" to refer to all who would include themselves as members.) The following breakdown is a useful starting point and others will have their own meanings for each letter. If the gay community is anything, it isn't of one mind! To fully appreciate each designation, keep in mind that these aren't fixed categories and they are representative only of those who self-identify as such.[1]

Lesbian: A woman who experiences the human need for warmth, affection, and love from other women.

Gay: A man who experiences the human need for warmth, affection, and love from other men. (Gay is often inclusive of the community, but in this acronym it stands for the male.)

Bisexual: A person who experiences the human need for warmth, affection, and love from persons of either gender.

Transgender: A broad umbrella term for persons who have a selfimage or gender identity not traditionally associated with their biological gender. Some transgender persons wish to change their anatomy to be more congruent with their selfperception, while others do not have such a desire. There is no absolute correlation between sexual orientation and transgender issues. A transgender person may identify as heterosexual, gay, lesbian, or bisexual.

Queer: Used by some to refer to themselves, the LGBT Community, a person who is LGBT, or even someone who is supportive of the LGBT communities. It's often viewed as a political statement as well as an identity. Many who use the term feel it is more inclusive, allowing for the diversity of race, class, ability and gender that

---

1   My thanks to Out Front Minnesota for these definitions. www.outfront. org/home

is represented by the LGBT communities. Caution: Many LGBT individuals dislike this word and view it as pejorative.

Intersexual: Generally applied to individuals born with ambiguous genitalia (an outdated and offensive term is: Hermaphrodite). In the past, most intersexual individuals have had surgery shortly after birth in an attempt to give them an "identifiable" gender. There is now much discussion about this practice, but so far little has changed. Parents often feel forced to make a quick decision with little information.

Questioning: There are those who aren't sure of their sexual orientation or aren't heterosexuals but nevertheless are unsure that their sexual orientation belongs in any of the above categories. These may include asexual persons.

Ally: A person, usually heterosexual, who supports and stands up for the human and civil rights of LGBT people.

What these all have in common is that none of these orientations was chosen, all are deeply imbedded in their being, and each is a viable way to live one's life. They all could be very fulfilling if they would be given a chance to be who they naturally are, without constraint or condemnation for being different. In fact, many have gone on to prove just that—in spite of the opposition that accompanies their every move. If ever a testimony to the value of being one's self (or living the way God made you) is needed, this is it.

LGBTs are as normal as normal gets— There is no need to "cure" them

Many parents feel responsible for their children not being "normal," due to the relentless propaganda, coming from the Religious Right and their allies, that tries to convince them that parents' behavior toward their children, especially distant fathers and overbearing mothers, produce gay children.

A few years ago I attended a lecture by Dr. Joseph Nicolosi, the chief proponent of this theory of homosexual origin and treatment, known as Reparative Therapy. After it was over, I asked him why I turned out to be straight when my parents fit the description perfectly. "Well," he said, "It doesn't always work that way." It sure doesn't, and for good reason. Every respectable professional association not only condemns this theory, but labels it positively harmful. It promotes needless guilt in parents and holds out false hope that gays can be "returned" to heterosexuality.

Here's a summary statement taken from ReligiousTollerance. org:[1]

> The American Psychiatric Association removed homosexuality from its list of mental illnesses in 1973. The American Psychological Association followed suit in 1975; the National Association of Social Workers in 1977; the National Psychoanalytic Association finally followed suit in 1991, stating that homosexuality was not a disorder. The American Academy of Pediatrics, American Counseling Association, American Association of School Administrators, American Federation of Teachers, American Psychological Association, American School Health Association, Interfaith Alliance Foundation, National Association of School Psychologists, National Association of Social Workers, and National Education Association formed the "Just the Facts Coalition." They developed and endorsed "Just the Facts About Sexual Orientation & Youth: A Primer for Principals, Educators and School Personnel" in 1999.

The primer says, in part:

> "The most important fact about 'reparative therapy,' also sometimes known as 'conversion' therapy, is that it is based on an understanding of homosexuality that has been rejected by all the major health and mental health professions. The American Academy of Pediatrics, the American Counseling Association, the American Psychiatric Association, the American Psychological Association, the National Association of School Psychologists, and the National Association of Social Workers, together representing more than 477,000 health and

---

1   http://www.religioustolerance.org/hom_expr.htm

mental health professionals, have all taken the position that homosexuality is not a mental disorder and thus there is no need for a 'cure.'"

The most important thing I believe that should be taken from these professionals is that there is absolutely nothing to be concerned about. Parents did nothing wrong, and LGBTs are perfectly normal. This is not to say that there will be no issues associated with gayness that they will have to face. However, these conditions are a product of society's ill-formed picture of what being gay is all about. Fortunately, they are diminishing at a rapid rate, so quickly in fact that now a majority of Americans believe that same-sex marriage should be legal.

Charles Darwin's conviction that the origin of sexual orientation is one of humanity's deepest secrets, available to no one, is still true. One thing is for certain, parents are not the reason for gay children. If there is a God, and I believe there is, God made us all the way we are.

Chapter 1 Discussion Starters

1. When did you realize there is more than one sexual orientation?

What made you aware?

2. What were your first impressions of homosexuality?

3. How much of your early information about homosexuality came from family, friends, or the media?

How much came from LGBTs?

4. Name some publically gay people who have impressed you the most. The least?

5. With all the evidence from scientific studies demonstrating that homosexuality is a normal human condition, why do you suppose people don't believe it?

THE GAY AGENDA:
WHY IT'S NEEDED
AND APPROPRIATE

*Things come apart so easily when they have been
held together with lies.*
~ Dorothy Allison, *Bastard Out of Carolina*

The fact that there is a gay agenda, at least on the part of the leaders of the Gay Rights movement, shouldn't be understood as anything out of the ordinary. All movements have agendas, including political parties, religious organizations and nonprofit enterprises like the Red Cross. So simply having goals they want accomplished shouldn't be off-putting. This is a normal function of modern movements that want to advance their causes.

However, many opponents of gay rights are trying to make it look like there is something underfoot akin to the subversive activities of the communists of the 1950s, along with a corresponding witch hunt. I hope to show that, regardless of the hysteria surrounding the reality of a gay agenda(s), these are reasonable, responsible and valuable contributions to the public square. (Notwithstanding the outlandish charges masquerading as part of the agenda, but are only made up by the opposition.) This is why I chose to feature a list developed by a critic of the Gay Rights movement, John Rankin, of the Theological Education Institute. It is a fair assessment of what he sees as the gay agenda, except for the last two, and will be analyzed below.

For some opponents of same-sex marriage—actually all things gay—the very survival of Western civilization is at stake; at the least, their notion of what Western Civilization should be. Others fear for the sanctity of the church. Still others worry about their families and the survival of the basic family structure that they understand to be the biblical model (but isn't). Their reactions to the forward progress that the Gay Rights movement has lately achieved range from hysterical (National Organization for Marriage) to measured (Liberty Education Forum).

There are two kinds of lists that purport to be the "homosexual agenda." One totally lacks restraint in its overreach. It claims that the bottom line of Gay Rights activists is to turn all our children into gays and lesbians. Some even go so far as to claim that they want all children to be their sexual objects and would do it if they could get away with it, as Scott Lively suggests in his book, *Why and How to Defeat the 'Gay' Movement.* Here's an excellent cautionary word from the Senior Pastor of Moody Bible Church, Erwin Lutzer, and Evangelical critic of same-sex marriage.

> So we have to remember that the radical gay community does not speak for all gays. When we read that NAMBLA, the North American Man-Boy Love Association, wants to lower the age of sexual consent to thirteen, and when a book is published that advocates sex with children, we must remember that the authors do not speak for all of the homosexual community. Indeed, such writers might speak only for a small fraction of it. If we don't like it when others paint us with a big brush, let's not do the same with the gay community.[1]

1   *The Truth about Same-Sex Marriage,* p. 49

Thank you, Dr. Lutzer.

I put John Rankin of the Liberty Education Forum in the latter category (measured), since the agenda as he sees it is mostly correct and evenhandedly stated. He is generally amiable and professes to love LGBTs, of which I have no doubt, yet he goes off the deep end with the final two. Here's his assessment of the homosexual agenda:[1]

Gay Rights activists want to:
1. Remove the concept of homosexuality as "sinful," and remove the concept that homosexual behavior is intrinsically unhealthy.

2. Define homosexual identity and behavior as a "normal" and healthy "variant" within the plurality of the human community, and call for "toleration" of it.

3. Move from "toleration" of it as a "normal variant," to a full "acceptance" of its intrinsic nature as being equal with that of heterosexuality.

4. Gain ecclesiastical, legal and social "approval" of the personal and social "goodness" of homosexuality, and call it "gay."

5. Translate this "approval" into leadership positions – especially ordination status in the church and political office in the culture.

6. Redefine "marriage" to include "same-sex" relationships.

7. Elevate "gay" relationships to a place of moral superiority for the wider culture to honor and emulate.

---

1   http://www.teii.org/marriage-or-pansexuality/an-eight-fold-agenda/

8. Define "homophobia," "hate speech" and/or "hate crimes" as the cardinal theological and political "sins," and remove the First Amendment liberties of anyone who disagrees, including those of ministers, rabbis and priests who refuse to perform same-sex marriage ceremonies; and at the extreme, remove the protection of unalienable rights for dissenters to this "new orthodoxy."

Let's look at each in their order.

Remove the concept of homosexuality as "sinful," and that homosexual behavior is intrinsically unhealthy

I don't know why he chose to keep "sinful" and "unhealthy" as one category, unless he is equating the two. Otherwise, they should be separate. This agenda item is necessary because many churches continue to categorize homosexual behavior as sinful and deserving of hell. Regardless, there is a considerable body of scholarship defended by world-class biblical scholars that would not understand homosexuality as sinful. Several denominations are now affirming same-sex unions and marriages as wholesome activities of the church, as well as portions of others. So I would affirm that leaders of the Gay Rights movement should have this item as part of their agenda. It is based on the recognition that homosexuality is a natural part of the human experience, and need not be characterized as aberrant any longer.

As for homosexual behavior being "intrinsically unhealthy," I offer a response that includes both male and female homoerotic acts from medical neurobiologist Jeramy Townsley:

> From a biological perspective, the idea that God clearly created male and female genitalia to be complementary is based on pseudoscience and not on an understanding of human anatomy and sexual physiology. The common argument from traditionalists is twofold: 1) God had one purpose in mind for sex—procreation; and 2) the male-fe-

male genital anatomy attests to the complementarity of God's intent for sex as solely for male-female/penile-vaginal sex (see Gagnon, *The Bible and Homosexual Practice,* 2001).

The most obvious argument opposed to the proposition of singular usage is that the penis was clearly designed to serve several purposes: procreation (depositing sperm), pleasure (has nerves associated with pleasure, the pudendal nerve) and for excrement of waste. One of Gagnon's primary claims to the "obviousness" of the misuse of the rectum for sex is that the rectum is a transport for excrement, however he fails to explain the distinction for the penis which clearly has both sex and exremental functions.

Further, the ano-rectal area also appear to be created for uses other than singularly for waste excretement.

It may or may not be merely coincidence that this area is the appropriate size and expandability to accommodate a penis (similar to the vagina). Despite Gagnon's claims, the medical evidence shows that ano-rectal sex does not produce muscule or pathological tissue damage to the area.

Just inside the male rectal canal is the prostate gland, stimulation of which heightens the sexual experience due to innervation with the pudendal nerve, the same nerve that innervates the penis.

Stimulation of the ano-rectal area and the prostate gland can alone produce orgasm in the male.

The vagina is obviously designed for multiple purposes--procreation and pleasure (innervation by the pudendal nerve). Contrary to traditionalist theologies and patriarchal cultures (including many cultures that practice female circumcision) that have ignored the sexuality of women as irrelevant, non-existent or evil, the biological fact that the vaginal area is innervated with nerves associated with pleasure, it would seem clear that God intended the vagina to be used not just for men, but primarily for women.

While vaginal penetration is important to many women for sex, current research on the female orgasm is turning away from penetration as the primary stimulant for sexual arousal and satisfaction, to the clitoris, laying on the surface of the vagina, therefore not requiring penetration, indicating that God may have created women (by design) to be able to experience sexual satisfaction outside of penetrative sex.

Most of the authors who oppose the various forms of gay sex based on biological issues fail to address similar types of sexuality between heterosexuals, including married couples. Many actively support oral sex between heterosexuals, quite common among both heterosexuals and homosexuals. Gagnon, for instance, quotes a Rabbinical text allowing for oral sex between heterosexuals (p.

299). Further, many of these authors fail to condemn heterosexual anal sex, which many studies
have shown is not an uncommon form of sexual intimacy between heterosexuals. The question
then becomes why issues of "nature" and biology
can be used to condemn homosexuality based on
anatomical issues while not subsequently limiting
heterosexual sex to penile-vaginal sex.[1]

I don't expect those whose minds are made up to immediately
change their minds with exposure to the evidence and logic of this
data. I do expect that they will find room, at least in this instance
(so far), that there is another side to this debate which can no longer
be characterized as totally without merit.

Define homosexual identity and behavior as a 'normal' and healthy 'variant' within the plurality of the human community, and call for 'toleration' of it

This item combines the second and third items in John
Rankin's list of the gay agenda.

If homosexuality were, indeed, an unhealthy aberration of the
human condition, it shouldn't be tolerated. We should do all we
can to alleviate the condition and bring its victims as much relief
as possible. If the above agenda items were pursued by means of
propaganda and false science with the goal of making something
aberrant seem justified, then it would be acting responsibly to oppose it. But this is far from the case.

There have been many in very responsible positions who
championed the Gay Rights cause in and out of the scientific community. Over the last 50 years, all the major psychological and
psychiatric professional organizations have investigated the subject
of homosexuality from every possible angle and determined that
homosexuality is a normal and healthy variant within the plurality

---

1   http://www.jeramyt.org/gay.html#ad

of the human community. Here is a representative statement from the American Psychological Association:

Is homosexuality a mental disorder:

> No, lesbian, gay, and bisexual orientations are not disorders. Research has found no inherent association between any of these sexual orientations and psychopathology. Both heterosexual behavior and homosexual behavior are normal aspects of human sexuality. Both have been documented in many different cultures and historical eras.[1]

Despite the persistence of stereotypes that portray lesbian, gay, and bisexual people as disturbed, several decades of research and clinical experience have led all mainstream medical and mental health organizations in this country to conclude that these orientations represent normal forms of human experience. Lesbian, gay, and bisexual relationships are normal forms of human bonding.[2]

Therefore, these mainstream organizations long ago abandoned classifications of homosexuality as a mental disorder.

The APA goes on to state that the only real problem associated with homosexuality is the unwarranted stigma that some in society wish to perpetuate, and the deleterious effects this can have on individuals.

Given the overwhelming documented results of the research, it can be affirmed that homosexuality is a normal, albeit, minority sexual orientation, and that it, in itself, engenders no mental health risks to homosexuals. By virtue of this, it must be considered a respectable orientation along with heterosexuality, and bisexuality, and toleration of gays and lesbians is the least we can do as a society.

---

1   http://www.apa.org/helpcenter/sexual-orientation.aspx
2   http://www.apa.org/helpcenter/sexual-orientation.aspx

Ultimately, LGBTs deserve full acceptance and integration into all aspects of life. To do any less is to perpetuate the last respectable bigotry in America.

As an agenda of the LGBT community, it is a legitimate and hugely successful agenda item. Because it is the right thing to do.

So we are now left to wonder why it is that some continue to perpetuate the now outdated and ill-informed notions that gays and lesbians should be shunned, reprogrammed, even persecuted. Gay bashing is still done across America, and violence continues to be directed at them.

One statistic jumps out at those of us who wonder: It is the most religious Christians who are the most hostile to gay rights and marriage equality.[1] That is, the most conservatively religious. We shouldn't wonder when Sunday after Sunday their parishioners get inundated with antigay messages. Just as with the global warming deniers, who deny it in the face of overwhelming evidence to support it, and with 98% of all climate studies agreeing, churches continue to pedal antigay "scholarship" that no respectable seminary or university would tolerate. There is no safe harbor for these deniers; they are all occupied by people of good will who are armed with first rate evidence and no longer sit on the sidelines.

Yes, the professional academy has moved well past tolerance and is now accepting LGBTs as rightfully a part of our world and is working diligently to get the proper information out.

Gain ecclesiastical, legal and social "approval" of the personal and social "goodness" of homosexuality

Again, (combining numbers 4 and 5 in Rankin's list) these are perfectly legitimate pursuits. It only seems strange to those who react negatively to the arrival of LGBTs in their places of worship. But there is little that can be done for such as these. They will continue to accept the pronouncements from their pulpits and tightly run synods and denominations that the only possible reason

1   http://www.gallup.com/poll/159089/religion-major-factor-americans-opposed-sex-marriage.aspx

a Christian would associate with gays is to have the opportunity to "save" them. They will continue to close their ears to the volume of biblical scholarship amassed over the last century that clearly shows that, for those who have eyes to see, LGBTs rightfully hold their claim as Christians.

The fact that many openly gay clergy have been ordained, even promoted to high office, signifies the success that the movement enjoys in promoting this part of their agenda. The election of Gene Robinson as Bishop of the Episcopal Diocese of New Hampshire and Mary Glaspool as Bishop of the Episcopal Diocese of Los Angeles are just two of many LGBTs who have ascended to high office of late. Also, the Presbyterian Church (USA) and the Evangelical Lutheran Church in America have recently voted to end their longstanding prohibitions on openly gay clergy members. The United Church of Christ and the Unitarian Universalist church have ordained openly gay clergy for decades. Add to that the many congregations that will ordain and call openly gay pastors, the success of mainstreaming LGBTs in the church and society is apparent. Give this agenda item its rightful due: it has succeeded and succeeded well.

The removal of the Sodomy laws was a major step in advancing this agenda item. On June 26, 2003, the U.S. Supreme Court in a 6-3 decision in *Lawrence v. Texas* struck down the Texas same-sex sodomy law, ruling that this private sexual conduct is protected by the liberty rights implicit in the due process clause of the United States Constitution. Ironically, many of those crimes defined as sodomy were widely practiced by heterosexual couples, and continue to be. How people consensually choose to express their sexuality is deemed not a matter of governmental concern and increasingly isn't seen as anyone else's, either.

Also ironically, the uneven enforcement against LGBTs, overlooking the widespread breaking of sodomy laws by straights, was a major reason for striking down the law. So the striking down of this law had as much to do with gay opponents' overzealous abuse of the law as the proponents of gay rights fighting these laws in court. No matter. This aspect of the agenda is accomplished. Still to come are, gay adoption, and the removal of all laws allowing discrimination against gays on the job.

Social approval was accomplished due to the widening acceptance of homosexuality as a normal part of the human experience. Part of this was due to the research by the profession organizations that clearly shows that LGBTs are as normal as the next person. But, the overwhelming verdict in favor of gay acceptance came when our sons and daughters, parents, uncles and aunts, cousins, pastors, friends and coworkers, and the person in the next pew, revealed their sexual orientation in large numbers. When people came face to face with the true face of homosexuality, their fears vanished, their love for them continued, and the desire for full access to all the rights any other human is afforded became their cause, too. They are no longer strangers to be feared, but the very person they've always loved and admired.

I say to you who see only gay exhibitionists, and think pedophiles are gay (they are not!), and hear only from homophobic ranters, open your eyes! You are surrounded by gays who you actually admire and don't even know it. That's how normal they are. Imagine if heterosexuals were all thought to be like the Mardi Gras revelers or the nightly visitors to the singles bars, and the people displayed on porn sites. But we know there is a wide world of straights and gays who far outnumber these and continue to live conventional lives. That's why the agenda is working.

Redefine 'marriage' to include 'same-sex' relationships.

As will be reviewed below, the redefinition of marriage has been a continuous pursuit over many millennia. Marriage has never always been between one man and one woman, as many critics of same-sex marriage would have us believe. They have recently modified it to say that it has always been a matter of opposite sexes marrying, and even that is false. True, same-sex marriages are rare among Western societies, but they are found even today. Their bottom line position has become that, well, Jesus was in favor of only one man and one woman marrying, so we should be too. That is a far cry from their original position that it has always been that way.

Not all biblical scholars and theologians agree that Christian marriage can be only between one man and one woman. (Many Christian missionaries allow converts in polygamous marriages to continue in them, without barring them from baptism or communion.)

It is one thing to say there is a norm and quite another to say that that norm is universal. It is the norm that most humans are right handed, but it isn't universal. It is the norm that most Mexicans speak Spanish, but not a universal. It is the norm that Christian heterosexuals are expected to marry the opposite sex, have children, and not divorce. As I say, this is the heterosexual norm. But what of nonheterosexuals? How can they be expected to conform to a norm that isn't possible for them?

As much as the critics of the gay agenda would like to believe that America is a Christian nation, it isn't. Israel is a Jewish nation, Saudi Arabia is a Muslim nation, but the USA is a democratic republic, presided over by the Constitution. So whatever Christianity may say or not say, its rules for itself are confined to itself and are prohibited from being forced on an unwilling public (insofar as it is unwilling). Therefore, to insist, rightly or wrongly that the Bible says marriage can only be between one man and one woman, we respectfully say, you have no standing in this decision. It isn't for you to decide.

What the Supreme Court of the U.S. wrestled with isn't what the Bible says about marriage, but what does the Constitution tell us we must do with respect to same-sex marriage and the Defense of Marriage Act. Youth entering high school are astonished to learn from their history of the United States that marriage between separate races was once illegal in many parts of our nation. It is virtually unthinkable that as late as 1964, states could prohibit two people in love, but of different races, to marry. Interestingly, these same students are on record as overwhelmingly in favor of same-sex marriage. Do you suppose there is a connection? Known injustices have a way of translating outrage against other injustices.

The Mexican Supreme Court on February 19, 2013, produced an opinion that makes same-sex marriage legal in some parts of their country. Interestingly, they cited the logic of the U.S. Supreme Court in its striking down of laws banning interracial marriage. Here's the part of the Mexican court's opinion that bears on our point:

> The historical disadvantages that homosexuals have suffered have been well recognized and documented: public harassment, verbal abuse, discrimination in their employment and in access to certain services, in addition to their exclusion to some aspects of public life. In this sense ... when they are denied access to marriage it creates an analogy with the discrimination that interracial couples suffered in another era. In the celebrated case Loving v. Virginia, the United States Supreme Court argued that "restricting marriage rights as belonging to one race or another is incompatible with the equal protection clause" under the constitution. In connection with this analogy, it can be said that the normative power of marriage is worth little if it does not grant the possibility to marry the person one chooses.[1]

It may be that SCOTUS returns to its own logic in the Loving case and ends one more inequitable slice of American life and makes same-sex marriage legal across the nation.

I have to believe (the evidence is just too obvious) that the reason so many people fight against this inequality is that they really don't believe that LGBTs deserve equal standing with heterosexuals. That they are somehow less than human, even, and to grant them this right would be to dignify the undignifiable. The Roman Catholic Church considers LGBTs "intrinsically disordered." Those who are Christians and feel this way justify themselves, often, with the belief that anyone who is destined to hell shouldn't be afforded any heaven on earth. What a pity.

---

1   http://ireport.cnn.com/docs/DOC-930304

But many other Christians, who fight daily for the realized dignity of LGBTs, look to the day when no one is denied their rightful place in that great community called humanity—even in the church as well as in the nation and world.

Elevate 'gay' relationships to a place of moral superiority for the wider culture to honor and emulate

So far, each of what Rankin identifies as the gay agenda I uphold as not only true, but welcome in a free society. However, this item goes beyond anything that the mainstream gay leadership has proposed. Rather than "elevating 'gay' relationships to a place of moral superiority," they merely want to level the playing field; they are after simple equality with heterosexual rights and privileges.

Here's a representative sampling of such goals:

In a 1987 speech to the National Press Club in Washington, homosexual spokesperson Jeff Levi remarked, "We are no longer seeking just a right to privacy and a protection from wrong. We also have a right — as heterosexual Americans already have — to see government and society affirm our lives."

In an article entitled "Gays on the March" in 1975, Time magazine quoted gay activist Barbara Gittings who stated: "What the homosexual wants, and here he is neither willing to compromise nor morally required to compromise—is acceptance of homosexuality as a way of life fully on a par with heterosexuality."

The only way the gay rights agenda can be exploited by its opponents to include more than simple equality is to parade the fringe elements that don't speak for the majority. It's like saying the Republican Party is for killing abortion doctors because those killers have been conservative Republicans. Or that Democrats are soft on defense because some peaceniks are Democrats. Any representation that goes beyond wanting homosexuality to be considered anything other than as normal as heterosexuality is a straw man that easily draws the uninformed to the side of the dissenters.

So far I have not used the word homophobia. I have avoided it, not because it doesn't exist, but because it too easily reduces the opposition to an easy target, which is what straw men are for. Yet, it is true that those who are viscerally opposed to homosexuality will use any means whatsoever to bolster their prejudice. They will look for the most absurd or extreme form of an argument to hang their hat on. I'm convinced that much of the hysteria surrounding the gay agenda amounts to that. The ideas that gays want to turn all children into homosexuals, that all child molesters are gay, that gay teachers are a threat to our children, that free speech is opposed by gay leaders, that gays are out to destroy the traditional family, and the like, aren't supported by the experts who have given their lives to the study of these issues, nor are they a part of the broad consensus of leaders. They are lies that are packaged with seemingly good evidence, yet lack factuality.

Conspiracy theories abound. The "gay threat" is the perfect combination of atmospherics that lend themselves to conspiratorial thinking. When you don't like gays, don't know many gays, don't trust gays, are afraid of gays, and think they tend to congregate together in dark places, you can imagine most anything is possible. They are labeled abominations, deviants, psychologically disturbed, intrinsically disordered. They allegedly hate themselves, hate the Bible, distrust Christians, and mostly meet in bars. What are they up to? What's going on when they are secreted away? There are those who still believe that the moon landing is a hoax and that Elvis is alive, and that the gay threat is the most urgent concern for Americans. There is nothing that can be done for these folk. As more and more LGBTs "come out," it's discovered that they are much more like everyone else than not, wanting no more than what any respectable human wants, and deserves to be treated as such. The day is coming, and very quickly, when the rest of this foolishness will be seen as silly as having ever thought that races shouldn't intermarry.

**Define "homophobia," "hate speech" and/or "hate crimes"
as the cardinal theological and political "sins," and
remove the First Amendment liberties of anyone who
disagrees, including those of ministers, rabbis and priests
who refuse to perform same-sex marriage ceremonies;
and at the extreme, remove the protection of unalienable
rights for dissenters to this "new orthodoxy"**

This assertion purporting to be a universally held item of the gay agenda has all the earmarks of a red herring to divert attention from the original issue. Here is how a politically conservative blog presents the issue:

> Gay marriage will end up infringing on religious freedom. The moment gay marriage becomes the law of the land, all sorts of First Amendment freedoms involving the free exercise of people's religion will likely be infringed upon as a consequence. No pastor should be forced to marry a gay couple. No wedding photographer, cake maker, caterer, or wedding planner should be forced to be involved in these weddings. No church or any other location should be forced to be the site of a gay wedding. Children will be taught in schools that gay marriage is normal, legal, and moral—and it directly contradicts the teachings of Christianity, Judaism, and Islam. To create this special privilege for gay Americans would mean impinging on the First Amendment rights of more than 200 million Americans.[1]

Nowhere in this posting is there any referencing as to how these rights will be infringed upon. The weasel phrase "likely be infringed upon" is not only weak, it is an admission that there is really no basis for the fear. As for no "pastor should be forced to marry a gay couple," no pastor will be. Anyone familiar at all with the doctrine of Separation of Church and State applied to the U.S. Constitution should know that there is nothing to fear here. Some appeal to the experience in Canada following the legalization of same-sex marriage in 2005.

---

1   http://townhall.com/columnists/johnhawkins/2012/02/17/five_reasons_
    to_oppose_gay_marriage/page/full/

Teachers are particularly at risk for disciplinary action, for even if they only make public statements criticizing same-sex marriage outside the classroom, they are still deemed to create a hostile environment for gay and lesbian students. Other workplaces and voluntary associations have adopted similar policies as a result of their having internalized this new orthodoxy that disagreement with same-sex marriage is illegal discrimination that must not be tolerated.[1]

Two things of note. One, this is about CANADA, not the United States of America. They have very different laws and traditions concerning freedom of speech and religion. And their decade long experience shows that earlier aggressive actions to enforce their law have abated and the law is in great favor throughout the country. To date, 68% favor the law and only 18% oppose it.[2] And in the United States, the Supreme Court upheld the right of the infamous Westboro Baptist Church to picket funerals with signs declaring "God hates fags," in *Snyder v. Phelps*.

However, as to "No wedding photographer, cake maker, caterer, or wedding planner should be forced to be involved in these weddings," we shall have to wait and see. Do recall that restaurants, theaters, hotels and the like which serve the public were compelled to integrate following the Civil Rights Act of 1964. It is only right that we protect all minorities from the oppression of the majority whenever and wherever it is found. As much as opponents want to characterize this as "special privileges," it is merely granting another group facing profound discrimination equal protection under the law. We will not only learn to live with this imposition of the state, but who would want to turn back to the days of Jim Crow and

---

1   http://www.thepublicdiscourse.com/2012/11/6758/
2   Based on the Canadian Forum Research poll of 2012. http://bayobserver.ca/canadian-same-sex-marriage-by-the-numbers/

legal segregation? (Oh, yes, they are around, but they've turned their hate to other things.)

And, yes, children will be instructed in schools about things LGBT, just as their parents were taught as children about the whys and wherefores of integration, the equality of the races, the harm of discrimination, and the need to accept differences for the sake of all. The churches may, if they wish, continue to teach that homosexuality is an abomination, and others will counter that God did make Adam and Steve. Funny, just as the news from the conservative right is full of horror stories about the coming ill effects of gay acceptance, and especially of same-sex marriage, so the pulpits and airwaves of the 1950s and '60s warned that integration would be the end of America as we know it, and the end of the freedom to practice Christianity as we see it. Well, it was the end of America as we knew it. Thank God.

Chapter 2 Discussion Starters

1. Has your understanding of the goals of the Gay Rights movement changed over the years? If so, how?

2. Does the gay agenda as reported in this chapter strike you as reasonable? Why or why not?

3. What items in the gay agenda do you have a problem with, if any? Why?

4. Did Jeramy Townsley's research give you new information? Was it helpful?

5. Why do you suppose more conservative Christians have difficulty accepting homosexuality as normal?

6. Should the United States Supreme Court take the Bible into consideration? Why or why not?

7. Why do opponents want to exaggerate the goals of the Gay Rights movement? Do you think they have?

8. How did life change in America after the ending of Jim Crow segregation? Were people's rights affected? How might America change if same-sex marriage becomes the law of the land?

THE CLOSET:
PRISONERS OF HETEROSEXISM

*Nor—at the most basic level—is it unaccountable
that someone who wanted a job, custody or visiting
rights, insurance, protection from violence, from
"therapy," from distorting stereotype, from insulting
scrutiny, from simple insult, from forcible interpretation of their bodily product, could deliberately
choose to remain in or reenter the closet in some or
all segments of their life.*
~ Eve Kosofsky Sedgwick,
The Epistemology of the Closet

There is no doubt that "the closet" is the most harmful result of continuing to deny LGBTs a legitimate and equal place
in society. By not acknowledging them, heterosexuals force them
into hiding. The results are often catastrophic. What is also not
in doubt is that the closet is of heterosexual making. Rather than
wag fingers and preach condemning sermons, everything should
be done to eliminate this despicable situation. If the closet doesn't
result in actual death, it severely limits its occupants' choices for a
full life and reduces them to living contrary to their best impulses.

This simple fact remains: If the closet is eliminated, all those things that are negatively associated with gayness disappear as well.

Here are just a few of the negative results:
Clandestine and anonymous sexual practices
Inappropriate marriages
Self-loathing (internalized homophobia)
Susceptibility to disease (STD and otherwise)
Truncated sense of wholeness (disempowerment)
Superficial relationships with straights and gays
Imposed hypocrisy
Sheer pain of not being oneself
Intense loneliness of not having a life companion openly at one's side

Let me be perfectly clear: the closet is created, welcomed, and maintained by straight people solely for their benefit. Because they make life miserable for nonheterosexuals, they are driven into secrecy, into the closet. They live lives that hide their true identity from the world. There, they are forced to live lives of such bewildering complications that it's amazing that any can pass as straight. This "out of sight, out of mind" mentality doesn't make it go away, it complicates life for everyone.

In this chapter, we will be taking a look at the devastating consequences of closeted living. My hope is that it will convince people of good will that whatever problems anyone may have with the so-called "gay lifestyle," heterosexuals are the cause and must assist in the cure.

It is true that the population of the closet is getting smaller and smaller, due in large part to LGBTs coming out in large numbers. As strides are made in all aspects of society that bring the unsubstantiated charges against LGBTs to light, and the misinformation peddled by uninformed people is replaced by solid research, the pressure to hide is lessened. Yet the closet is by no means a thing of the past. Therefore, much work still needs to be done to make it possible for our closeted citizens to feel that they can live as free to be themselves as anyone else.

Heterosexism, the Begetter of the Closet

I ask you, if you are a heterosexual, do you ever…

…fear holding hands with your lover in public?

…fear your sexuality will be held against you at work?

…reject thoughts of having children and grandchildren out of hand?

…get apprehensive upon leaving a straight bar?

…hide your sexual identity from your family and friends?

…send out false signals regarding your sexual identity to appear otherwise?

…think that your heterosexuality is a burden in any way?

Or do you…

…remember fighting against your initial fears you may be heterosexual?

…loathe yourself for being "unnatural"?

…resent your feelings of attraction to the opposite sex?

…keep your sexual identity from your friends and family for fear of rejection or condemnation?

…often wish you were not heterosexual?

…ever consider entering therapy to try to reverse your heterosexuality?

…hope that your sexuality might someday be accepted, but never imagine it would be held in high esteem?

…live deep in the closet because you are afraid to live openly as a heterosexual?

Of course, Mr. or Ms. Heterosexual, you never were confronted by any of these situations. You have lived your life free from the burden of orientation pretense and openly pursued your life. How very different from our LGBT friends and family members.

In order to keep their jobs, their standing in social circles (including churches), even their sanity, they feel they must keep their true sexual orientation hidden. For if they don't, the personal and economic consequences are often very harsh, even life threatening. It's no wonder many choose to live a closeted existence.

So, just what is it that set up such conditions that LGBTs feel it necessary to hide? It is called heterosexism.

Heterosexism is an enculturated system of bias regarding sexual orientation. It encourages values in favor of heterosexual people and enforces prejudiced actions against LGBTs.

In other words, heterosexism is a means by which heterosexuals maintain their power. It is not unlike white racism in that regard.

Gregory Herek, professor of psychology at the University of California, distinguishes between two manifestations of heterosexism:

> Cultural: The stigmatization, denial, or denigration of nonheterosexuality in cultural institutions ranging from the church to the courthouse.

> Psychological: A person's internalization of this worldview which erupts in antigay prejudice and homophobia.[1]

Virtually every society has in-groups and out-groups. For keeping minorities subjugated to the dominant culture, two operations are used: prejudice and discrimination. This results in the singling out of individuals or groups of people as targets of hostility even though they may have little or nothing to do with the evils for which they stand accused. Scapegoating is the result, with the closet as the only defense against heterosexism and homophobia.

1   G. M. Herek, (1990). "The context of anti-gay violence: Notes on cultural and psychological heterosexism." *Journal of Interpersonal Violence*, 5

This is why heterosexuals are responsible for creating and maintaining the closet. They like it that way. They maintain their power and keep opposition at bay.

How do heterosexuals further the heterosexist agenda? In ways both overt and covert. "That's so gay," supports the notion that a heterosexual shouldn't show signs of the opposite sex. "You throw like a girl," indicates that males with feminine traits are less than heterosexually masculine. "Marriage should be restricted to one man and one woman," reinforces the heterosexual privilege. "The Bible condemns homosexuality," puts nonheterosexuals in their place. "If you must have a same-sex relationship, keep it in private," means gays aren't entitled to the freedom afforded to straights. We could extend this list indefinitely.

I once referred to myself as an "avowed heterosexual." I said it in response to someone who referred to another as an avowed homosexual, as though that was too horrifying to contemplate. We went on to discuss heterosexual privilege. I asked him why it was okay for him to show affection to his wife in public, but not for gays. I asked him why we aren't allowed to discriminate in job hiring and housing against racial minorities, but it is perfectly fine to discriminate against gays. I asked him why we (used to) keep straights in the military, but give gays bad conduct discharges. I asked him why straight couples are allowed to adopt children, but in most states, gay couples cannot. I asked him why sodomy between straight couples was fine, but not with gay couples. You get the picture; that's heterosexism doing its work.

The tendency of straights is to blame the situation on gays and attribute these offenses to their moral inferiority. However, the stark reality is that, by virtue of heterosexism, straights created each and every condition that is so easily condemned when the accusing finger should be pointing back at them. Straight people of good will throughout the world are realizing the harm the closet perpetuates and are working diligently to dismantle it. Why not; they made it in the first place.

Ill-considered marriages

By making life miserable for LGBTs, many resort to the secrecy of the closet in order to protect themselves. To do so, they must appear as normal sexually as everyone else seems to be. Often, this involves getting married. Often, at least two lives are ruined in the process. If children are involved, the body count continues. People being forced into unnatural marriages is one of the most devastating aspects of the closet.

You don't have to look too far to know of such marriages. I know of many. A dear friend of mine had his wife come to him in tears, sobbing out, "God made me wrong." They ended up divorcing. Thankfully, no children were involved.

Another friend and pastoral colleague learned of his wife's lesbianism when an affair was uncovered. This time, children were involved.

An elder in a church I served married and had a child. He couldn't live what he termed "a lie," and eventually ended his marriage.

These stories could be continued indefinitely because they are all around us. Just reading them on the page doesn't come close to the heart wrenching trauma suffered by all involved. Broken hearts, ended dreams, lives turned upside down, and children bewildered. These are but a few of the consequences of forcing people to live contrary to their nature. If you want to get a real sense of the anguish that comes with this, watch the documentary, *For the Bible Tells Me So*. It is available on Netflix.

The truly frustrating aspect of this is that it is totally unnecessary. If there were no closet, there would be no need for these marriages in the first place. And if same-sex marriage were available and acceptable, first marriages would be starting out as they should. More and more people are seeing the logic of this and are now supporting efforts for gay normalization.

Recall that the first "not good" following all that was good in the creation stories of Genesis was that the man was alone. God said, "It is not good for the man to be alone." It is also not good for a man or woman to be forced into a marriage that maintains this loneliness. For only that partner who truly is suitable can end such loneliness. For nonheterosexuals, only a same-sex partner will do.

I don't want to indict the motives or the character of those who make the choice to try to live their lives as best they can by trying to conform to society's expectations. Many actually start out believing that they will somehow change by getting married, only to realize, too late, that they can't change. Others feel they are in love with their marriage partner, but discover that it is the love of a friend, not a spouse. Still others discover their true sexuality after marriage. Many who are still married but unhappy (lonely) persevere because of religious scruples and live lives of quiet desperation. I don't wish to disparage any of them for the choices they make, for it is a situation forced upon them by a heterocentric society that offers no good alternatives. If you truly regret this situation, you need to do all you can to make the closet no longer necessary.

To deny same-sex marriage is to deny one's humanity

For most of us, our families are the center of our lives. We live in constant awareness of and with high purpose for those we call family. We hardly do anything outside of work that doesn't involve them, directly or indirectly. Few decisions we make are made without reference to their well-being. And if we are happily married, our spouse is the most significant person in our life.

But for those who live their lives in the closet, who marry for the sake of self-protection, or who chose to remain single, life lived without the most satisfying relationship a human may enjoy, loving and being loved by a deeply devoted life partner, is denied them.

For Christian LGBTs, this is a heightened problem, for the church, almost universally, condemns any effort they might take to relieve the loneliness that constantly dogs them. Out LGBTs have found satisfying life partners and live lives not much different from straight couples, enjoying the ebb and flow that accompanies all relationships. But closeted LGBTs, Christian or not, are denied such a life.

What is being asked of Christian nonheterosexuals is punishing. Richard B. Hays, in his *The Moral Vision of the New Testament*, writes,

> Heterosexual persons are also called to abstinence from sex unless they marry (1 Cor. 7:8-9). The only difference, admittedly a salient one, in the case of homosexually oriented persons is that they do not have the option of homosexual marriage. So where does that leave them? It leaves them in precisely the same situation as the heterosexual who would like to marry but cannot find an appropriate partner (and there are many such): summoned to a difficult, costly obedience, while groaning for the redemption of our bodies (Rom. 8:23).[1]

Gay Christians, according to Hays, are essentially no different from single heterosexuals whom the church teaches that premarital sex is wrong and counsels them to remain virgins until they are married. But, straights and gays are far from being in precisely the same situation, because the heterosexual— let's call him Greg— has the hope, even the strong possibility of someday being married. Greg can hope, and hope makes all the difference for him. But Norman, a gay man, has no hope. He is denied the possibility of ever having his greatest need met—a loving partner openly accompanying him through life. Asking him to be chaste for life is not a natural condition, and this spiritual gift is rarely granted. Even when it is, it isn't without its challenges.

Let us be clear about this. What is demanded of Norman is not merely to deny himself sex. It is demanded of Norman that he deny his humanity. The effect is the suicide of Norman's spirit. This I find to be profoundly unchristian and unworthy of a compassionate God.

More and more congregations and denominations are finding this situation needlessly burdensome for their LGBT members and are holding marriage ceremonies for them. In many cases, these are

---

1   p. 32

marriages "in the sight of God" only, as the state has yet to legalize them. But they are, nevertheless, just as fulfilling to the gay couples as any straight marriage can be, at least spiritually.

But the closet is still the enemy of those it continues to house. As long as they remain safely inside, the possibility of a complete life is beyond their grasp. They will languish, continuing to seek furtive, incomplete alliances which will only remind them of what they will never have. Their human longing for the one who can make all the difference in their lives will go unabated. They shrivel and die. As one who left the closet for good told me, "The oxygen in there grew thin and I could hardly take a breath. I was suffocating to death."

> The biblical command to love one's neighbor, to treat her as the "sacred animal" (Lactantius) that she is, creates binding duties for the Christian....The obligation to love our neighbors in a manner commensurate with their sacred worth and responsive to their vulnerability and neediness creates a Christian duty to intervene on their behalf when their worth is being isolated, their core needs are going unmet, or their vulnerability is being exploited.[1]

The sooner the nation and church make marriage available for nonheterosexuals, the sooner will the loneliness of the closet and its consequent inhumanity be eliminated. After all, doesn't the Golden Rule, "Do to others that which you would want done to you," demand that? Imagine for a moment, if you are straight, life without your significant other. Why should anyone else be forced to live that way?

---

1   David P. Gushee, *The Sacredness of Human Life*

Chapter 3 Discussion Starters

1. How does this chapter describe "the closet" as a prison? Is it a fair comparison?

2. If you are straight, how did you react to the "fears" list at the beginning of the chapter?

3. How is heterosexism similar to racism?

4. In what ways have you observed how heterosexism is maintained?

5. Can you blame LGBTs for living in the closet?

6. What can be done for reducing the need for the closet? Will it ever be eliminated?

7. In what ways does heterosexism deny gays their humanity?

8. What's the difference in the quality of life for Greg and Norman?

THE (EVOLVING) HISTORY OF MARRIAGE

*Like it or not, today we are all pioneers, picking our
way through uncharted and unstable territory. The
old rules are no longer reliable guides to work out
modern gender roles and build a secure foundation
for marriage. Wherever it is that people want to end
up in their family relations today, even if they are
totally committed to creating a so-called traditional
marriage, they have to get there by a different route
from the past.*
~ Stephanie Coontz, *Marriage, a History*

When was the last time you heard of a man actually asking the
intended's father for her hand in marriage? Even better, if asked and
denied, did it really make any difference? The wedding would most
likely have gone ahead without the father's permission.

This quaint courtesy is a holdover from the days when fathers
actually controlled the destiny of their daughters (and sons, for
that matter). Marriage only recently has become the business of
the couple alone. In the days of the Patriarchs, in and out of the
Old Testament, the father arranged for spouses for his children, and
unless there was a need for a special alliance outside the immediate
family, they were often first cousins, even half-sisters or brothers.
The purpose of marriage was to continue the name of the father

through his sons, to provide assistance for managing the family property and protection in old age.

Another quaint custom not often heard of these days is the "hope chest." Young women would store away items for their household, such as linens, a trousseau, and other finery, for their new home with their (hoped for) husband. This was the final remnant of the "dowry" that figured into ancient and early modern marriages. Marriageable women would show their desirability as a marriage choice by the contents of their dowry. Since most women were covered from head to toe, were secreted away from most men, and had little opportunities for getting to know them were available, the dowry served instead.

A man could have several wives and concubines. (Jacob married two sisters, Leah and Rachel, and Solomon had 700 wives and 300 concubines.) Women were normally permitted only one husband at a time. In the case where a young married woman became a widow, the brother of the dead husband was bound to marry his sister-in-law, and provide her children, or be humiliated by the community. This is known as levirate marriage.

Divorce was easy and only the husband's prerogative. All the Old Testament husband had to do was find something "unclean" in his wife and he could write a bill of divorcement and she was kicked out of the house. What this unclean thing was, isn't known. In Jesus' day, the two central rabbis had differing opinions. Hillel said that offering burnt toast was a sufficient cause for divorce; Shammai said it must be a serious offence like adultery.

Even the marriage ceremony is a modern invention. Several stories in the Old Testament emphasize that the husband simply took the bride into his tent, verified her virginity, had sexual intercourse, and she lived with his family from then on. There was no religious ceremony involved. And if the bride was discovered not to be a virgin, she was to be stoned to death.

In the West, it was not until the reign of Caesar Justinian, C.E. 527-565, that laws regulating marriage were put in place. Contracts were drawn up between families according to Roman law, and courts would decide the legality of certain marriages and divorces. The lower classes basically practiced "common law" marriages, because they had little or no property to fight over.

Religious interest in marriage is late

Until the ninth century marriages did not involve the church. Up until the twelfth century there were blessings and prayers during a ceremony that may or may not have been related to a church. Then priests asked that an agreement be made in their presence. It was only then that religion was added to the ceremony. It became a sacrament in the 16th century by action of the Council of Trent.

Until the late 19th century and early 20th century, marriage was more of a necessity than it is today. Today men don't need women to run a household, or bear them children for labor on the farm, or to obtain a dowry. Women don't need husbands to provide for their livelihood, or for bearing children, or for status in society. Marriage these days is for none of the reasons of yore.

So marriage today is quite different from marriage in Bible times or even relatively recently. It has evolved from being strictly an agreement between family patriarchs, involving a man and one or more wives, to a free will decision between two consenting adults. And in these twelve states, Connecticut, Delaware, Iowa, Maine, Maryland, Massachusetts, Minnesota, New Hampshire, New York, Rhode Island, Vermont, and Washington—as well as the District of Columbia— marriage is legal between two people of the same sex. More states are poised to join them in the near future.

Although marriage has usually been between a man and one or more women, it has normally been an opposite sex institution. There have been cultures where women were able to marry more than one man, and where people of the same sex were allowed to marry.[1] It isn't possible to say with authority, as many try to, that marriage has always been between one man and one woman, or even opposite sexes.

[1] For a cursory history of accepted same-sex unions, see http://
  en.wikipedia.org/wiki/History_of_same-sex_unions

All of this is to say that marriage is always evolving. There was even a time when incest was considered appropriate, where sons and daughters were forced to marry even those who were strangers, where marriage was for the convenience of the father at the expense of the daughter, where love had nothing to do with it. There is likely no period before our own in which any of us would have liked to live under their marriage laws or customs. It took us centuries, even millennia, to arrive where men and women are free to choose their partners. Well, that is, if you are heterosexual. If you are not you are still subjected to rules, in most states, that no one else wants to live under. For that reason alone, all people should be afforded the ability to marry the one of their own choosing.

Jesus on marriage

The first observation about Jesus and marriage that is often overlooked is Jesus never married. This is significant for several reasons; the major one will be dealt with later. But for now, let us just note that, for his time, to be a healthy man and remain single was considered loathsome. On the face of it, they thought such a person was willfully violating God's demand that humans procreate. And Jesus would soon be at the age where peasant Palestinian men usually died, thus limiting his prospects for a family. He obviously opted out of the traditional family. This could have something to do with the charge that he was a "drunk and glutton." He wouldn't be given the benefit of the doubt. He even took up the habits of the similarly loathsome Cynics[1], well known throughout Galilee, who had no visible means of support, lived off others, believed in "free love," and traveled in groups which included women. I am not suggesting Jesus was a Cynic. I am saying that he easily could be accused of being one by his contemporaries. Such was his disregard for the conventional way of living.[2]

---

1   http://en.wikipedia.org/wiki/Cynicism_

2   *Who Is Jesus?: Answers to Your Questions About the Historical Jesus,* edited by John Dominic Crossan, Richard G. Watts, p. 90

So, Jesus can't be held up as the standard bearer for the Christian Right's notion that the ideal (Christian) man is married and the head of his household, with his subordinated wife and children trailing along behind. There is no place to go to for Jesus' example of a good husband. And let's not appeal to the theological metaphor of Jesus as the bridegroom to the church-as-bride. The marriage is not until after "the new heaven and new earth" is here, where "there will be no marriage or giving in marriage." The most we can say is that Jesus had a very long engagement. Marriage is a temporary, earthly institution in which Jesus did not participate. Why that is the case is significant.

Actually, both Paul and Jesus thought marriage was not the ideal situation for Christians. This passage from 1 Corinthians 7 sums up Paul's thoughts on the matter:

> I want you to be free from anxieties. The unmarried man is anxious about the affairs of the Lord, how to please the Lord; but the married man is anxious about the affairs of the world, how to please his wife, and his interests are divided. And the unmarried woman and the virgin are anxious about the affairs of the Lord, so that they may be holy in body and spirit; but the married woman is anxious about the affairs of the world, how to please her husband. I say this for your own benefit, not to put any restraint upon you, but to promote good order and unhindered devotion to the Lord.

> If anyone thinks that he is not behaving properly towards his fiancé, if his passions are strong, and so it has to be, let him marry as he wishes; it is no sin[1]. Let them marry. But if someone stands firm in his resolve, being under no necessity but having his own desire under control, and has determined in his own mind to keep her as

---

1   Often overlooked in commentaries is that this indicates that the Corinthians may have held the belief that to be single was a sin, and Paul is clarifying this for them by stating unequivocally that it is not.

his fiancé, he will do well. So then, he who marries his
fiancé does well; and ***he who refrains from marriage will
do better:*** [Emphasis mine]

Paul would prefer that everyone be single, or behave as single, as he himself was. For him, not marrying is the ideal for both
men and women. Yes, Paul did believe that Jesus would return in
his generation to set up the Kingdom of God on earth, and this
tempered his concern for other things as well, such as slavery. Yet
this goes to my point that marriage is a contingency subject to the
needs of the day, not a necessity of one kind for all time.

Jesus has a similar view (of Kingdom timing and of marriage),
and this is likely why Paul felt the way he did. Here is how Matthew
reports Jesus' thoughts on the matter:

> They said to him, 'Why then did Moses command us to
> give a certificate of dismissal and to divorce her?' He said to
> them, 'It was because you were so hard-hearted that Moses
> allowed you to divorce your wives, but at the beginning it was
> not so. And I say to you, whoever divorces his wife, except for
> unchastity, and marries another commits adultery.'

> *His disciples said to him, 'If such is the case of a man with his
> wife, it is better not to marry.' But he said to them, 'Not everyone
> can accept this teaching, but only those to whom it is given. For
> there are eunuchs who have been so from birth, and there are
> eunuchs who have been made eunuchs by others, and there are
> eunuchs who have made themselves eunuchs for the sake of the
> kingdom of heaven.* **Let anyone accept this who can.'** *[Emphasis
> mine]* (Matthew 19:7-12)

Both Paul and Jesus recognize that being single is very difficult, even impossible for some who would sin sexually otherwise.
So marriage is actually a lesser state than being single. Paul urges
everyone to consider staying single, and Jesus urges anyone capable
of living single to do so.

It is clear that whatever purposes marriage used to serve, in
the Christian age it is for the purpose of allaying sexual sin. For

both Jesus and Paul, procreation has been set aside as a lesser value and both marriage and children are an encumbrance to spreading the gospel. Marriage is decidedly not the be-all and end-all of life that needs to be protected at all costs. It is a contingency for the time being that will not be found in the afterlife. This explains why marriage was not emphasized from the beginning in Genesis and was allowed to be culturally derived for millennia. In the biblical view, God has no particular stake in it, other than it be proscribed by the Golden Rule, as all relationships are to be guided.

So, you can see that allowing same-sex couples to marry isn't so consequential that marriage can't be adjusted to accommodate it, as marriage customs have changed to accommodate human need down through the millennia. And LGBTs need marriage for all the same reasons that straight people need marriage. There are very few Jesuses and Pauls in our world. For the rest of us, marriage is the answer.

Yes, marriage changes, and it should change to accommodate the increasing awareness of overlooked, yet needed, aspects of our life together as a human community.

Chapter 4 Discussion Starters

1. Can you think of other ways marriage has changed? What has changed even in your lifetime?

2. Were you surprised that the church's interest in marriage is relatively late? Why do you suppose that was the case?

3. What are the most pressing forces against marriage stability today?

4. Can Jesus really be used as the defender of "traditional marriage"? Why or why not?

5. How do you feel about conducting religious marriage ceremonies without the benefit of state sanction?

6. Some people are advocating for the state to regulate only civil unions for all couples, straight and gay alike and leave "marrying" to religions institutions. What's your opinion?

THE CASE FOR
MARRIAGE EQUALITY

*If I truly value your humanity, then I will value
your most precious relationships....What does it
mean if I steadfastly refuse to honor your spouse?
Your children? Your family? At a basic level, it
means that I do not honor you. I am denying something essential about you, your identity,
your right to belong.*
~ David Gushee, *The Sacredness of Human Life*

The history of the United States can be summarized quite ac-
curately as the slow but sure realization of the vision of its founding
document, the Declaration of Independence. The Declaration said,
"All men are created equal," yet the Constitution said, "Slaves shall
represent 3/5 of a human being." It also denied women the right
to vote, gave states the freedom to establish a religion, and upheld
"separate but equal" Jim Crow laws, making interracial marriages
illegal and restricting immigration to maintain white supremacy.

The founders had something in mind when they wrote the
Constitution, but it isn't the republic in which we now live. In fact,
their prejudices went so deep that they didn't even feel the need
to write "all white, landed, protestant, heterosexual, free men are
created equal." Forget about their slaves, forget about people with
other creeds who would later emigrate, forget about women, forget

about those without land, forget about gay people—the only ones who had the right to vote, and thus the right to participate in the building of this new republic, were men exactly like them.

In the intervening years, slavery has been abolished, women have been fully emancipated and nonwhites have been given the full dignity of the law. The unalienable right to life, liberty and the pursuit of happiness for all Americans is now the realized dream of that distant day.

There is, however, one notable and continuing exception: nonheterosexual Americans.

It is my contention that withholding marriage rights for nonheterosexuals is unconstitutional, unchristian, and un-American. I will make the case for same-sex marriage being beneficial to America by providing four bedrock reasons why same-sex marriage rights deserve to be placed on par with heterosexual marriage rights.

Same-sex marriage is good for America because it is a justice issue that needs to be resolved

Americans are seekers of justice for all. As Dr. Martin Luther King Jr. said many times, "If there is injustice anywhere, there is injustice everywhere." That is why his widow, Mrs. Coretta Scott King, said on many occasions that, if Dr. King were alive today, he would be fighting hard for gay rights. It confounds me that the daily violence, job and housing discrimination, defamations and insults, occasional murder, and spiritual condemnation heaped upon nonheterosexuals, due simply to their sexual orientation, does not automatically qualify them as an oppressed class. Let's remember that in scripture God always takes the side of the oppressed over that of the oppressor.

But I take solace in remembering the other struggles for justice in America. It was not self-evident that slavery was wrong. It took nearly 100 years from the founding of our nation to recognize this injustice and right this wrong.

It was not self-evident that segregation was wrong. Nearly another one hundred years was needed to rectify it.

It was not self-evident that anti-miscegenation laws were oppressive. As recently as 1967, with *Loving v. Virginia,* we finally eradicated this injustice, allowing interracial marriages in America.

It was not self-evident that women should have the right to vote. But we realized the error of our ways and enfranchised women after 150 years of marginalization since the ratification of the Constitution.

We could add to this list many other examples of oppression in American history: immigrants, most non-Christian religions, especially Judaism and even Roman Catholicism (the original targets of the Ku Klux Klan), and non-Europeans who were banned from entering the country. It didn't require a constitutional amendment or court order to rectify these oppressions. America managed to overcome most of these biases and eventually incorporated these formerly oppressed peoples into the American mainstream.

Again, I take solace in America's ability to recognize our oppressive attitudes and actions and rise above them. But we need to remember that in each of these cases, the oppressor turned to Scripture for support. After all, Paul did write in the New Testament "Slaves, obey your earthly masters with fear and trembling, as you obey Christ" (Ephesians 6:5).

Levitical prohibitions such as not planting two different kinds of seed in the same field, not cross-breeding animals, or wearing garments of two different kinds of material woven together, were seen as biblical justification for keeping the races segregated.

They were also used to keep blacks from marrying whites. I once heard a Southern preacher say during the days of Jim Crow, "You don't see sparrows mating with crows, or rattlers mating with water moccasins. Neither should we be mixing negroes and whites. Oh, yes they are all birds, and all snakes, and all humans, but God has commanded that we reproduce 'by our own kind': Whites with whites and negroes with negroes."

The realization is finally dawning that it's time to face up to the oppression of nonheterosexuals. Progress began in small ways when certain municipalities passed non-discrimination ordinances in housing and jobs, when states passed hate crimes legislation and civil union laws. Businesses realized that if they were to compete for the best employees they would have to offer protections and benefits to nonheterosexual employees and their partners. As recently as 2003, the United States Supreme Court struck down all sodomy laws, and today, in twelve states plus Washington, D.C., same-sex marriage is legal.

All this progress has not come easily. Each advance has been met with the same opposition America's oppressors have always employed: Biblical condemnation, the manufacturing of phony statistics to demonstrate moral inferiority, and spreading lies, such as that gay men are all child molesters, and that they will harm our children by turning them into homosexuals.

The oppressors want people to believe that the fate of the nation is bound up in this cultural war against nonheterosexuals. In effect, they are saying: If America loses the traditional identity of the nuclear family our nation is doomed.[1]

The Bible is much more a friend to LGBTs than it is their enemy. Gays and lesbians, bisexuals and transgenders are as normal and as law abiding—even as conventional—as most heterosexuals. In addition, the widely praised nuclear family is really a very modern way of doing family. The Christian Right would have you believe that this is the biblical model. They wish us to believe that marriage has always been "one man, one woman, one lifetime." All you have to do, however, is read a few chapters into the Bible to find that Abraham had more than one wife, as did his son Isaac, and many other prominent Old Testament characters. Both Jesus and Paul authorized divorce and remarriage.

---

1   See for example Alan Caruba's blog: http://www.teapartynation.com/
     profiles/blog/show?id=3355873%3ABlogPost%3A1018343&xgs=1&xg_
     source=msg_share_post

The question is not: Will America survive the inclusion of nonheterosexuals into its mainstream? Of course it will. No, the appropriate question is: Can America be America if it does not end its oppression of gay Americans? Will we become a nation that is willing to endure second-class citizens after two centuries of steady emancipation of other oppressed groups? I believe that America's soul is at greater risk by this moral failure. This is a justice issue that needs to be addressed and resolved in favor of the oppressed. Offering same-sex marriage is the final step in recognizing the full, unencumbered humanity of nonheterosexuals and their inclusion as fully emancipated American citizens.

Same-sex marriage is good for America because it is consistent with the evolution of marriage

America will benefit by an expanded understanding of marriage.

If America truly followed the biblical laws regarding marriage, it would look something like this:

~Marriage in the U.S. shall consist of one man and one or more women. (Genesis 29:17-28; 2 Samuel 3:2-5)

~Marriage shall not impede a man's right to take concubines. (2 Samuel 5:13; 1 Kings 11:3)

~A marriage shall be considered valid only if the bride is a virgin. If the bride is discovered not to be a virgin, she shall be executed. (Deuteronomy 22:13-21)

~Marriage of a believer and a non-believer shall be forbidden. (Gen 24:3; Numbers 25:1-9; Ezra 9:12; Nehemiah 10:30)

~Since marriage is for life, neither the U.S. Constitution nor the constitution of any state shall be construed to permit divorce. (Deuteronomy 22:19; Mark 10:9)

~If a married man dies without children, his brother shall marry the widow and impregnate her. (Genesis 8:6-10; Deuteronomy 25:5-10)

Oh, but you say the New Testament eliminated some of these undesirable aspects of marriage. Yes, indeed. This is another way of saying that marriage has evolved, isn't it. And if Jesus' attitude toward marriage and the family is examined, it is far from the presumed biblical model of marriage currently touted by leaders of the Christian Right.

In times past, marriage provided for a woman's security, children for household and farm labor, old-age security for parents, the maintenance of power through family alliances, and a supply of first-born children dedicated for service to the church. Until recently, marriage was of convenience, and based on societal mores, not of love.

All of these reasons are irrelevant for why people marry today. If we want children—adoption, en vitro fertilization, surrogate mothers, are all available today with little cultural inhibition. Social Security, Medicare and pension plans have replaced children as guarantors of old age survival. Few households need child labor to survive; in fact, we have laws that prohibit such exploitation.

Theologically, marriage has evolved. The early patriarchal cultures of the Bible attached no religious significance to marriage. A man simply took his woman to his tent, verified she was a virgin, and they were married.

It comes as a shock to many that there was nothing like a marriage ceremony for the 1200 years of Christianity, even though it eventually became a sacrament of the church.

Augustine worked out a theology of marriage in the 5th century that came to dominate Western Christian understandings of marriage well into the Middle Ages. Augustine saw marriage as an office. It became a way in which one served the church and the larger society.

According to Dr. Tex Sample, this office serves three ends:

> ~The procreative end. For Augustine, this involved raising children for the sake of the Church. It is not primarily for the purpose of claiming progeny as one's own.

~The unitive end, in which couples learn faithfulness to each other and to Christ, and thereby become witnesses to an "order of charity."

~The sacramental end. This becomes his basis for the indissolubility of marriage.[1]

The emergence of the Reformation altered these ends considerably. Today procreation is downplayed due to the population crisis, the unitive end is seen as support for mutual fidelity and sexual enjoyment, and the sacramental end is no longer observed.

Since the late 18th century in America, marriage has been largely defined as a civil contract between two people who choose to live together in loving fidelity. Procreation has ceased to be necessary for marriage to be held in esteem.

The point is this:

> Marriage in the Christian tradition serves a number of ends: procreation, fidelity, sacrament, mutual support, loving companionship, and enhancement of society. What is striking is that all these ends can be met by homosexual marriages. This is even true of the procreative end if the procreative end is understood as raising children for the Kingdom of God and not primarily as a function of nature [a biological function]. On these grounds, it is appropriate for gay and lesbian Christians to be married in the church and not be in violation of Scripture or tradition.[2]

Same-sex marriage is good for America because it offers no downside

The standard response to this statement is that same-sex marriage demeans the institution of marriage and is an assault on heterosexual marriage values.

---

1   http://www.gaychurch.org/gay_and_christian_yes/the_bible_christianity_and_homosexuality_justin_cannon.htm

2   http://www.gaychurch.org/gay_and_christian_yes/the_bible_christianity_and_homosexuality_justin_cannon.htm

Let me suggest that heterosexuals have done quite well on their own in demeaning the institution of marriage without any help from nonheterosexuals. Quite apart from being married by an Elvis impersonator in Las Vegas, the 55-hour marital jaunt of Britney Spears, the self-confessed 10,000 sexual partners of Wilt Chamberlain, or the one extramarital partner of Kobe Bryant, heterosexuals are guilty of a wide range of assaults on marriage. It is well known that the greatest threats to marriage today come from poverty, spousal abuse, unfaithfulness, drugs, and easy divorce. It seems to me that our energies would be better spent fighting in these trenches.

So, same-sex marriage is a convenient scapegoat for the many failures of heterosexuals. It is also a red herring to divert attention and to raise money. Here's a frantically written e-mail I received from Dr. James Dobson of Focus on the Family. He wrote,

> Dear Steven, This is an absolutely crucial letter because the institution I created Focus on the Family to preserve—the family— is not only under attack as it has never been before: It is on the verge of extinction." (He then appeals to me to contact my congressional representatives, ending with) "Thank you for your continued partnership with Focus on the Family and for taking a bold stand for marriage and the family—before there is nothing left to support. Sincerely, James Dobson, Ph.D.[1]

In this communication and in all others I have seen and received, there are never any concrete reasons given for why same-sex marriage is seen as harmful to heterosexual marriages. It is simply harmful by definition. Certainly, marriage will be changed because of same-sex involvement, but only for the better.

---

1   I was on their mailing list, but not, as you might imagine, a partner.

Same-sex marriage is good for America because it is a stabilizing influence on society

There is every reason to believe that marriage would be good for nonheterosexuals for the same reasons it is good for heterosexuals. After all, people are people. Nonheterosexuals want to be married for the same reasons heterosexuals do. If the Christian Right's stereotypical view of nonheterosexuals is true—that they are lust driven, orgy seeking, diseased in mind and body, incapable of monogamy—why on earth would they be interested in marriage? The fact is, they have every normal person's desire for the state of matrimony and for all the right reasons. Typically, all they want is the recognition that they are human beings. Therefore, the withholding of marriage to them (and in my mind, also) is the equivalent of withholding their humanity. It is the equivalent of making them 3/5 of a human being.

Here's a statement that I think we can all agree with. It's from a book entitled, *The Case for Marriage: Why Married People Are Happier, Healthier, and Better Off Financially*. It is co-written by Linda Waite and Maggie Gallagher. They sum up the case for marriage in this way:

> "New marriage partners together create a shared sense of social reality and meaning—their own little separate world, populated by only the two of them. This shared sense of meaning can be an important foundation for emotional health." Ordinary, good-enough marriages provide the partners with a sense that what they do matters, that someone cares for, esteems, needs, loves, and values them as a person. No matter what else happens in life, this knowledge makes problems easier to bear....

> "Marriage and family provide [a] sense of belonging . . . the sense of loving and being loved, of being absolutely essential to the life and happiness of others.

> Believing that one has a purpose in life and a reason for continued existence, (that life is worth the effort because one's

activities and challenges are worthy), come from having other people depending on you, caring about you. Married people have a starring role in the lives of their spouses; their shared universe would cease to exist if something happened to one of them. When the shared universe includes children, the sense of being essential, of having a purpose and a full life expands as well. Marriage improves emotional well-being in part by giving people a sense that their life has meaning and purpose....

"As Professor Normal Glenn stated in a critique of text-books, 'Most social scientists who have studied the data believe that marriage itself accounts for a great deal of the difference in average well-being between married and unmarried persons. Indeed, loneliness is probably the negative feeling most likely to be alleviated simply by being married....'

"The key [to well-being] seems to be the marriage bond itself: Having a partner who is committed for better or for worse, in sickness and in health, makes people happier and healthier. The knowledge that someone cares for you and that you have someone who depends on you helps give life meaning and provides a buffer against the inevitable troubles of life."

So the question becomes— why would anyone want to keep such a wonderful way of life solely for oneself and those like oneself, for heterosexuals only? Why not share this amazing institution with any who wish to honor its intentions and benefit from it? Why not, indeed.

Chapter 5 Discussion Starters

1. Why do you suppose Mrs. King believes that her husband would be supporting marriage equality today?

2. How are the Gay Rights movement and the Civil Rights movement comparable as legitimate pursuits?

3. What's the strongest case for marriage equality? The weakest?

4. Why is procreation as a necessary requisite for marriage not persuasive?

5. Do you agree with Waite's and Gallagher's high view of marriage? Why or why not?

FALSE CLAIMS REGARDING GAYS AND SAME-SEX MARRIAGE

The conventional view serves to protect us from the painful job of thinking.
~ John Kenneth Galbraith

Imagine (if you are straight) that you are about to enter a room full of strangers. You know nothing about them except one thing: they are gays, lesbians, and bisexuals with a sprinkling of transgender men and women. Do you walk in confidently, with the self-assurance of a person who is intimately acquainted with the gay community? Or, are you apprehensive about your ability to know your way around the room? Perhaps you are suddenly stricken with an anxiety attack not knowing what to expect and thinking the worst.

If you find yourself in the latter category, you aren't alone.

Now let's say, instead, that the room is full of Rotary Club members. How do you feel now? I suspect that the last thing you would worry about is an anxiety attack.

What's the difference? Easy; you likely know a great deal more about Rotarians than you do about the gay community. And what you think you know about the gay community might be informed by rumor, stereotypes, Gay Pride parades, Dykes on Bikes, Act Up and a plethora of propaganda from the Religious Right, such as

Focus on the Family and, well, pick a TV evangelist. It's no wonder you may be apprehensive at the least and mortified at worst.

The closet and the creation of stereotypes

Way back in 1965, in a CBS documentary, viewers heard Mike Wallace say,

> "The average homosexual, if there be such, is promiscuous. He is not interested or capable of a lasting relationship like that of a heterosexual marriage. His sex life, his love life, consists of a series of one–chance encounters at the clubs and bars he inhabits. And even on the streets of the city—the pick-up, the one night stand, these are characteristics of the homosexual relationship. And the homosexual prostitute has become a fixture in the downtown streets at night."

One thing we have learned since then is that this is not the picture of the "average homosexual." Not then or ever. It is, however, a slice of gay life that is also not all that uncommon among straight singles. But typical, no.

People back in that era were unfamiliar with the "average homosexual" because most lived deep in the closet. There was no way of knowing the totality of the community as it was hidden from view; at least, from straight view. All most people knew was based on rumor, innuendo and stereotypes passed from generation to generation. The "average homosexual" was as unreal as the Cleaver family's depiction of the "average family" on "Leave It to Beaver." Even in our time, when the closet is beginning to empty out, it is impossible to estimate the true percentage of the homosexual population because so many remain unnoticed.

Today we know that the broad outlines suggested in the CBS documentary are decidedly false. There are many thousands of documented faithful, life-long gay relationships, many of which became officially recognized in marriage ceremonies in states when they became legal. There are also innumerable Christian LGBTs who have persevered in their churches, even rising to high office as bishops, pastors, elders, deacons, teachers, choir directors, organists, as well as faithfully active members. Many who were raised in homophobic environments became supporters, even advocates of gay equality, when they got to know many LGBTs and discovered the stereotypes they were taught are manifestly wrong.

False claim #1... A gay's lifespan is shortened by 25-30 years due to a promiscuous sexual lifestyle

This is one of the most pernicious myths circulating about the gay community, and particularly about gay men. If even 10% of what is circulating as fact about LGBTs were true, I would not be writing this book. But after spending over twenty years in their company, I remain their friend and ally because I watched my false impressions fall, one by one, into an embarrassingly large cache of discarded assumptions.

If you aren't familiar with Dr. Paul Cameron, you likely have been influenced by his work. Here is what purports to be the results of a scientific study led by him, a supposedly reputable researcher. He asked:

> How long did homosexuals live before the AIDS epidemic and how long do they live today? We examined 6,737 obituaries/death notices from eighteen U.S. homosexual journals over the past thirteen years and compared them to obituaries from two conventional newspapers.

> The obituaries from the non-homosexual newspapers were similar to U.S. averages for longevity: the median age of death of married men was seventy-five, 80 percent died old (65 or older); for unmarried men it was fifty-seven, 32 percent died old; for married women it was seventy-nine, 85 percent died old; for unmarried women it was seventy-one, 60 percent died old. For the 6,574 homosexual deaths, the median age of death if AIDS was the cause was thirty-nine irrespective of whether or not the individual had a Long Time Sexual Partner [LTSP], 1 percent died old.

For those 829 who died of non-AIDS causes the median age of death was forty-two (41 for those 315 with a LTSP and 43 for those 514 without) and <9 percent died old. Homosexuals more frequently met a violent end from accidental death, traffic death, suicide, and murder than men in general. The 163 lesbians registered a median age of death of forty-four (20% died old) and exhibited high rates of violent death and cancer as compared to women in general. Old homosexuals appear to have been proportionately less numerous than their non-homosexual counterparts in the scientific literature from 1858 to 1993.

The pattern of early death evident in the homosexual obituaries is consistent with the pattern exhibited in the published surveys of homosexuals and intravenous drug abusers. Homosexuals may have experienced a short lifespan for the last 140 years; AIDS has apparently reduced it about 10 percent. Such an abbreviated lifespan puts the healthfulness of homosexuality in question.[1]

This summation of Cameron's "research" was pulled from his organization's website after receiving scathing denunciations from peer reviewed journals. He now offers an equally nonsensical explanation at www.familyresearchinst.com. Due to this and other spurious "results," Cameron had his memberships revoked by the Nebraska Psychological Association, and The American Psychological Association.[2] In a court case, *Baker v. Wade,* a District Court Judge called Cameron's sworn statement, "fraud."[3]

If this study were to be believed, we would have much to fear for our gay friends. But it is not to be believed; rest easy.

---

1   http://www.familyresearchinst.org/2008/12/the-longevity-of-homosexuals-before-and-after-the-aids-epidemic/

2   http://psychology.ucdavis.edu/rainbow/html/facts_cameron_sheet.html

3   The exact statement: "There has been no fraud or misrepresentations except by Dr. Cameron, the supposed 'expert' for District Attorney Hill."

False claim #2...Gays don't form loving relationships and are just interested in sex

Yet, the opposition continues trotting out so-called scientific studies which would keep in force these malicious stereotypes. One notable study is from Holland and is summarized in this way:

Homosexual Unions Last Only 1.5 Years, Says New Study

BY LIFESITENEWS.COM

• Mon Jul 14, 2003 11:15 EST

It also found that men in homosexual relationships have an average of eight partners a year outside their main partnership, adding more evidence to the "stereotype" that homosexuals tend to be promiscuous. The findings are "proof positive that these relationships ... will never be as stable as a normal heterosexual relationship regardless of what institutions or laws are changed," said Pete LaBarbara, senior policy analyst at Concerned Women for America's Culture and Family Institute, who predicts that homosexual promiscuity will remain "rampant."[1]

If this is all you had to go on, you might be inclined to take this at face value. However, what LifeSiteNews does not report is that this study was confined only to those who were treated at STD clinics, were 30 years and younger, may not have been in an actual relationship, excluded monogamous gay men, was confined to the city of Amsterdam, and open mostly to HIV/AIDS patients. In other words, this doesn't even begin to represent the gay community nor was it intended to. This study was limited to the promiscuous for the purpose of determining how AIDS spread in a community. And guess what they found? Non-monogamous gays aren't monogamous. I'm shocked, shocked! And, as far as lending

---

1   http://www.lifesitenews.com/news/archive//ldn/2003/jul/03071405

itself to conclusions about the "average homosexual," it totally left out lesbians.

According to an analysis in the Box Turtle Bulletin:

> This turns out to be a very common tactic among anti-gay extremists. Because they're eager to portray their positions as being backed by scientific research, they often turn to medical studies to support their arguments. And they are especially fond of studies of HIV/AIDS and other sexually transmitted diseases (STD's), which they can count on to provide especially juicy statistics to describe "what homosexuals do". But of course, all you really learn from these studies is what some homosexuals do—the ones who go to STD clinics because they've picked up a disease. By turning to Dr. Xiridou's study, these activists are following a well-worn path.

For a full review of the misleading interpretations of the Dutch Report, see this note.[1]

Now, to turn to the issue of promiscuity among gay men, let's not kid ourselves. Men, per se, are promiscuous. It is well-known among sociologists that women are the moderating factor in controlling male sexual urges. It is also true that the libido in men is stronger than in women. The following analogy is overly simplistic, yet to the point: Think of the libido as a light switch. For men, it is mostly on, for women it is mostly off. (Or, men are turned on and women need to be turned on.) Naturally, when men are attracted to each other, it doesn't take much for the libidos to take over. (I said this is overly simplistic, but not altogether unrealistic.)

But as to clandestine, anonymous sex, there may be a slight difference between gay and straight men. (Let's not overlook the fact that sex with prostitutes, phone sex, and one-night stands on the part of straight men, constitute clandestine, anonymous sex.) But why is it that gay men populate the bath houses, parks, and backrooms in bars, and cruise the streets looking for a willing partner? BECAUSE WHEN THEY ARE IN THE CLOSET, ANONYMOUS SEX IS ALL THAT IS AVAILABLE TO THEM.

---

1   http://www.boxturtlebulletin.com/Articles/000,003.htm

Yes, I am shouting. I am shouting because this reality needs to be clearly heard. It isn't because of moral laxity, or a character flaw, or an inherently deviant psychological disposition, but because as long as they are forced into the closet, they have no other choice. At least it seems that way to them. For to live one's gay sexuality in the open isn't an option for those who live in the closet.

False claim #3... LGBTs can change their sexual orientation back to heterosexual[1]

The ex-gay movement, as it is called, purports to include thousands of former homosexuals in its ranks. The cure rates published make it seem like change is possible and happens regularly under the supervision of a properly trained Reparative Therapy counselor. The truth, however, is far from it, and may be the most exploitive and harmful of therapies. Last year, California banned this type of therapy used on LGBT minors. Supporters of the bill, included California's Board of Behavioral Sciences and California Psychological Association. Critics have argued this therapy can cause debilitating emotional damage to patients.

Many of the so-called success stories are from highly motivated religious gays who believe that their orientation, if acted upon, will send them to hell. Now that's motivation to change! But leaders of the ex-gay movement actually are on the record saying that the most they can do for people is help them resist same-sex temptation. (See below)

Just as with sham marriages to keep one's reputation while living in the closet, many self described ex-gays have gotten married to opposite-sex individuals, only to finally admit that they are and will always be gay. In fact, several of the founding members of ex-gay organizations are included here.[2]

These would include Gary Cooper and Michael Bussee who were significant in the founding of the largest ex-gay ministry, Ex-

---

1   See also Chapter 7 and the section on 1 Corinthians 6:9-11.
2   Some estimates run as high as 3.4 million women have married or were married to gay men. Laumann, *The Social Organization of Sexuality.*

odus International. As chronicled by Wayne Besen of Truth Wins Out, "[T]he group was rocked to its core a few years later when Bussee and Cooper acknowledged that they had not changed and were in love with each other. They soon divorced their wives, moved in together and held a commitment ceremony."[1]

To counter the ex-gay movement, something called the ex-ex-gay movement emerged. It is populated by many of those who submitted to ex-gay therapy, claimed successful change to heterosexuality, realized that they were only fooling themselves, and resumed their gay life. However, this took a huge toll on their lives and many are still unable to deal with the hurt of the ex-gay movement. In June 2007, Bussee issued an apology at an Ex-Gay Survivors Conference to all of the people he helped get involved in ex-gay ministries.[2]

False *claim #4... Gays choose their sexual orientation*

Bear in mind that when it is noted that science can't explain the origin of homosexuality, neither can it explain the origin of heterosexuality. Both remain a mystery. There is much discussion and research around the "nature/nurture" debate that has people choosing sides, but no clear winner is yet to emerge. The evidence seems to be pointing to a combination of biology and environment.[3]

Here's the bottom line. The many times I've been challenged by someone who insists that it's a choice, I usually respond by asking, "If it's a choice, how easy would it be for you to make that change?" This is usually followed by a grimace and an unwillingness to continue the conversation. So, if this is what you believe, I ask you, "How easy would it be for you to change?"

---

1   http://www.truthwinsout.org/history-of-the-ex-gay-ministries/
2   http://www.truthwinsout.org/history-of-the-ex-gay-ministries/
3   http://allpsych.com/journal/homosexuality.html

False *claim #5…Gays are trying to convert straights into gays*

In the first place, conversion either way is impossible. We don't choose our orientations and can't move back and forth among them. So if anyone is fearful that gays are out to get their child, they have nothing to fear.

This item doesn't come from the gay community; it comes from the homophobic extremists using it as a scare tactic for resisting gay rights. Their chief instigator is Judith Reisman, currently visiting professor at the Christian Right's Liberty University. She has made a reputation, some say has become infamous, by her efforts to debunk Alfred Kinsey's research, even to the point of calling him a pedophile. Her whole thesis that homosexuals recruit, and target especially our children, is based on the fiction that gays know they choose to be gay. So the only way the pantry can be restocked, so to speak, is by getting the young to adopt the same choice. Else, the community will dry up and there will be fewer and fewer people to have sex with.

For a full analysis of Reisman and her crusade, read Poppy Dixon's report.[1] The lengths opponents take are astonishing. (By the way, you will be enlightened by Reisman's position that the Nazi's didn't really execute gays because they were actually gay themselves.)[2] See what I mean.

False *claim #6…Gays are anti-religious*

Here we go again. Antigay activists will stop at nothing including making things up or capitalizing on fringe elements to try to make them the rule, not the exception. This false charge is a case in point. No less that George Barna, an Evangelical Christian sociologist and researcher wrote the following in 2009:

People who portray gay adults as godless, he-

---

1 http://www.glapn.org/sodomylaws/usa/usnews118.htm
2 http://www.whale.to/b/reisman.html

donistic, Christian bashers are not working with the facts…. A substantial majority of gays cite their faith as a central facet of their life, consider themselves to be Christian, and claim to have some type of meaningful personal commitment to Jesus Christ active in their life today.[1]

Yes, there are groups such as Act Up, and individuals who protest churches for their intolerance and antigay teachings, even to the point of violence. Yet, to characterize a whole movement or people on the basis of the fringe is a serious breach of logic. It would be like saying that Fred Phelps and the Westboro Baptist Church (www.godhatesfags.com) are exemplars of mainstream Christianity. Gays would be much more in view in churches were they not subjected to frequent instances of antigay rhetoric and less subtle messages that they are not welcome. No wonder they are absent. Yet, I can tell you from years of listening to their yearnings, that many feel intensely the burden articulated by Augustine, that "We are restless, O Lord, until we find rest in Thee."

False claim #7… Same-sex marriage is a social experiment that will usher in the end of America

Glenn Stanton and Dr. Bill Maier, same-sex marriage critics, ask: "Why do we have to be so narrow in our definition of marriage?" They explain:

> Because nature is narrow in its definition of marriage, and for very good reason. . . . Nature does not tolerate very much diversity in the form of family, and any attempt to redefine marriage will be to our detriment. No society has ever prospered under a smorgasbord mentality of family life

---

1   Quoted in Chellew-Hodge, Candace. "New Poll Shows Gays and Lesbians Believe in God."*ReligionDispatches.* 25 June 2009

where people pick and choose forms that suit their individual tastes. To protect the common good, societies must enforce narrow parameters nature has given humans. Same-sex marriage will simply be the next chapter in a long line of failed social experiments with marriage and the family that have hurt people.[1]

Often those whose arguments include the death rate of civilizations try to include their favorite reason for decline, such as the above. An exact cause is virtually impossible to correlate because there is no one thing that brings down a civilization. There are always many causes at work. Additionally, all civilizations fail over time. Very few civilizations last more than a few centuries regardless of why, making the argument irrelevant.

No society has ever picked and chosen from a smorgasbord of possibilities for creating families. That certainly is not the case here with same-sex marriage. And nature is replete with examples of mixed families who raise their children together, the elephants being one example, with many of the females serving as mothers on a rotating basis.[2] In many cases with animals, dads often do the nurturing while mom hunts. And quite often, dads are non-existent following conception. This, along with Bagermihl, et al, conclusively demonstrates that nature is anything but narrow, and is no place to go for good examples for marriage and the family. Nature offers us anything but a narrow view.

False claim #8... Traditional marriages will be harmed if same-sex marriage becomes legal

The National Organization for Marriage uses their considerable influence to keep this claim alive. The following are a few examples of how they frame the charge pulled from their website.

---

1   Glenn T. Stanton and Dr. Bill Maier, *Marriage on Trial, p. 30*
2   http://www.andrews-elephants.com/family-structure.html#. UWRU05OZWSo

In answering the question, "Who gets harmed," these are the responses:[1]

> "The people of this state who lose our right to define marriage as the union of husband and wife, that's who. That is just not right."

> If courts rule that same-sex marriage is a civil right, then, people like you and me who believe children need moms and dads will be treated like bigots and racists."

> Religious groups like Catholic Charities or the Salvation Army may lose their tax exemptions, or be denied the use of parks and other public facilities, unless they endorse gay marriage."

> Public schools will teach young children that two men being intimate are just the same as a husband and wife, even when it comes to raising kids."

> When the idea that children need moms and dads get legally stigmatized as bigotry, the job of parents and faith communities trying to transmit a marriage culture to their kids is going to get a lot harder."

> One thing is for sure: The people of this state will lose our right to keep marriage as the union of a husband and wife. That's not right."

Let's take them one at a time.

Who gets harmed? Well, who bestowed the "right" to define marriage on you? As long as you believe that it's your right to impose your will on, now, the majority of Americans who believe same-sex marriage should be legalized, I guess you will feel harmed.

---

1   http://www.nationformarriage.org/site/c.omL2KeN0LzH/b.4475595/
     k.566A/Marriage_Talking_Points.htm. This page was recently removed
     from their website.

But it's not your right. Our rights are derived from the U.S. Constitution, not a self-appointed voice of authority.

The supposed loss of tax exemptions, etc. This is generally held by constitutional scholars to be a red herring. When New York legalized same-sex marriage, for example, they included broad protections for religious and charitable organizations that were actually found unnecessary, as the protections are inherent in the U.S. Constitution.

On the other hand, whenever minorities are granted rights long withheld from them, this means that the majority loses some of theirs. Hotels, restaurants and other businesses that serve the public are no longer able to discriminate on the basis of race, sex, or religion, regardless of how the owners feel. Gone are the "Whites Only" counters, "restricted clubs" (no Jews allowed), and red-lined neighborhoods. Most of us feel that whatever losses ensued is America's gain. Should the Supreme Court uphold same-sex marriage, life in America will go on pretty much as usual, with the exception that LGBTs will no longer be denied equal rights with the rest of us.

Just as schools had to begin to recognize the equality of the races, yes, equality of same-sex relationships with heterosexual relationships, including in the raising of children will be taught. Because it's true. The American Medical Association, the American Psychological Association, The American Psychiatric Association, and the Academy of Pediatrics all are on record as approving homosexuality as perfectly normal and as capable of entering any human relationship as any heterosexual.

This includes child rearing.

The American Academy of Child and Adolescent Psychiatry approved the following statement in support of gay, lesbian, bisexual and transgender parenting in 2009:

> All decisions relating to custody and parental rights should rest on the interest of the child. There is no evidence to suggest or support that parents who are lesbian, gay, bisexual, or transgender are per se superior or inferior from or deficient

in parenting skills, child-centered concerns, and parent-child attachments when compared with heterosexual parents. There is no credible evidence that shows that a parent's sexual orientation or gender identity will adversely affect the development of the child.[1]

I also concede that "the job of parents and faith communities trying to transmit a marriage culture to their kids is going to get a lot harder." I don't, however, view this belief in the importance of a mom and dad as bigotry unless it is advocated at the expense of nontraditional families. It is truly bigotry to label nontraditional families as dysfunctional, disordered or even pathological.

Finally, "The people of this state will lose our right to keep marriage as the union of a husband and wife...." True, again. However, I would insist on the phrasing as "presumed right." There is no loss of the ability for heterosexuals to marry the opposite sex. That will never change. That right will be forever intact. So nothing is really lost, but another very valuable right in America will be gained, the right of any person to marry the person of their choice.

False claim #9... Gay love is not the same as straight love

I'd like to introduce you to Bob and Frank. Bob and Frank met soon after they joined the Jesuit order of the Roman Catholic Church. In a memoir of their life together, Bob described how they each had walked similar paths, realizing at an early age that they would not have a conventional life, as, try as they might, they were not attracted to women. Being good Catholics, and wanting desperately to avoid the pangs of hell, as they were taught, they became servants of the church, giving up the possibility of life with a partner. However, the need for someone to fill their loneliness overtook them.

Here is how Bob describes the nature of their love for one another.

---

1   http://www.hrc.org/resources/entry/professional-organizations-on-lgbt-parenting

It was January 10, 1990. The week before we were test-
ed for HIV, but the Red Cross would not allow us to come
together for our test results. I was scheduled for the earlier
appointment. I went and received my test results of remaining
HIV negative. I was back home within fifteen minutes. Frank
left and did not arrive back promptly. My anxiety increased
geometrically with each five minutes, and after a half hour,
my anxiety turned to panic and tears. I knew in my heart the
truth of the situation and sobbed. When Frank arrived, his face
washed of color and filled with tears confirmed what I dreaded.
We wept together like Jesus at the tomb of Lazarus. We wept
for ourselves and for the dreams of our lives together. We never dreamed that one of us would be positive while the other
remained negative. Mixed antibody status was a near-death
experience for us, and we both began a grieving process at the
separation that was destined by those test results.[1]

All the passion, devotion, single-mindedness, power, unself-
ishness, and *agape'* love that we hope characterizes heterosexual
relationships are certainly found here. Bob's grief at the knowledge of the impending loss of his life partner is an emotion that
transcends sexual orientation and encompasses all humanity. It is a
part of all who have loved and lost, regardless of whom the object
of that love may be.

---

1   Robert Goss and Mona West, Eds. *Take Back the Word,* p. 211

Chapter 6 Discussion Starters

1. How comfortable are you around people different from yourself? How have you learned to become comfortable?

2. What notions have you had about LGBTs that have changed? What caused the change?

3. How many of the false charges have you heard repeated or seen in print?

4. Have you ever been susceptible to any of the misunderstandings in this chapter? If so, what changed your mind, if it changed?

5. Why do gay men get a reputation for promiscuity and not straight men?

6. How did LGBTs get the reputation for being anti-religious?

7. Why are some straight people convinced that same-sex marriage will hurt their marriage? Is there any basis to their fears?

7

BUT, MY BIBLE SAYS....

*You can safely assume that you've created God in
your own image when it turns out that God hates
all the same people you do.*
~ Anne Lamott

The ultimate recourse for those who want to keep homosexuality on the sins list is, "My Bible says...." The sentence generally ends with "...homosexuals are an abomination," or, "...gays are going to hell," or "…God hates gays." This is intended to be the final word on the matter; the Bible has spoken, the issue is clear, we can move on to other things. How so? Because the Bible has spoken.

The Bible, of course says no such thing. I will prove it to you. Go get your Bible. Now, take it in your hands and bring it up to your eyes. Say to it very clearly, "Bible, tell me, what do you have to say about homosexuality?" If you don't hear anything, repeat your question; maybe louder this time. If there is still no answer, shake it; it may be taking a nap. Still hearing nothing? Well, that's all right, because if you do hear the Bible answering, you may be on your way to a psychiatric hospital.

The Bible "says" nothing. It is an inert object, words on paper. It can't utter a sound. Of course, you knew that all along, yet you may still want to repeat that the Bible says something. What is really going on is that *people* say the Bible says something; people speak *on behalf of* the Bible. The Bible is deaf and mute.

Unfortunately, people too often make what "the Bible says" what they want it to say. You see, there is no such thing as an un-interpreted reading of anything, from the daily newspaper to the Bible. All of us read (or "hear what it says") though a filter or a lens. No one can read without one. Your filter/lens is everything that you have learned through your culture, ethnicity, gender, nation-ality, education...you get the point...that shapes how you perceive meaning. Every word you read or hear is processed through this filtering system. Everyone reads or hears the same word or words differently. Depending on how far apart our systems are, we can basically understand each other or totally misunderstand. In ex-plaining this to an adult Sunday School class, one member said, "I can think of something we both read that needs no filtering, that is straightforward and immediately understood." "Okay," I said. "Let's have it." He responded, "God is love." I replied with, "What do you mean by 'God' and what do you mean by 'love'"? He got my point.

When it comes to reading the Bible, we have a two to three thousand year old bridge to cross. We need to be able to "hear" as though we were an immediate member of the culture of those who created those biblical words. This is virtually impossible. The best we can do is approximate this; we will never actually achieve this. And even for those who were contemporaries, they had their own problems. Here's Peter's comment on Paul's letters: "There are some things in them hard to understand" (2 Peter 2:16). Indeed.

So the next time you are tempted to tell someone what the Bible says, why not be honest and tell them that you think this is what the Bible, properly interpreted, means. You will have achieved two things. First, you will have admitted that your interpretation is open to opinion (and that it is *your* opinion), and that you might be, dare I say it ... wrong.

We will now take a look at the few passages that have been interpreted as antigay.

Why God approves of Adam and Steve, as well as Adam and Eve

Maggie Gallagher quotes Norval Glenn in her book, *The Case for Marriage:*

> "Most social scientists who have studied the data believe that marriage itself accounts for a great deal of the difference in average well-being between married and unmarried persons. Indeed, loneliness is probably the negative feeling most likely to be alleviated simply by being married." (p. 77)

Gallagher and Glenn are on to something here. Loneliness is a universal condition which the Bible addresses from the very beginning. Human loneliness is at the heart of the marriage issue, although not well understood or articulated by either side. Ending human loneliness is crucial, not simply because it is an onerous human condition that no one unwillingly should be made to bear, but because it is the fundamental human predicament that first surfaced in the Genesis story of creation that caused God to reevaluate the human being.

From Genesis, Chapter 2, it is clear that God's first intention for the human being, *ha 'adam* was not heterosexuality or even sexuality, for *ha 'adam* was created as a "stand alone" being. In other words, no other creature was intended. Don't be confused by chapter 1 where in verse 27 we read, So God created humankind in his image, in the image of God he created them; male and female he created them. This is, of course, true (and obviates the overt patriarchalism of the story). However, it is a summary statement that concludes the events of Chapter 2, a much earlier story of creation than Chapter 1. So we need to read chapter 2 before the summary of Chapter 1 can make sense.

The story begins with God creating *ha 'adam* as someone who would be placed in charge of the garden, to care for and tend it with God as partner. For reasons not disclosed, God observes that it is not good for *ha 'adam* to be alone, and goes about making a suitable helper for him.

What happens next is unexpected and likely a surprise to some: the first thing God does to provide a suitable helper for the man is NOT to create a woman but to create animals and bring them to the man for his approval. Chapter 2:20 says, The man gave names to all cattle, and to the birds of the air, and to every animal of the field; but for the man there was not found a helper as his partner. We must take this seriously as an authentic effort on God's behalf to find for *ha 'adam* a suitable partner.

The first thing that strikes me about Genesis is that the picture of God's nature is very different from what I, as a young Sunday School student, was taught to believe. That God can be said to be omnipotent, omniscient, and omnipresent may be true, but having said that, one does not necessarily understand how it works out in reality. One of the longstanding arguments in theology relates to this: Does God know everything that will happen before it happens? (As with the Calvinists.) Or, does God limit God's omniscience to allow unhampered free will? (As with the Arminians.)

Interestingly, Genesis sides with the latter. On at least three occasions in the Torah God is found NOT to know the consequences of God's actions.

The first is found in Genesis 6:5

> The LORD **saw** that the wickedness of humankind was great in the earth, and that every inclination of the thoughts of their hearts was only evil continually. [6] And **the LORD was sorry** that he had made humankind on the earth, and it grieved him to his heart. [7]So the LORD said, I will blot out from the earth the human beings I have created people together with animals and creeping things and birds of the air, for **I am sorry that I have made them**." [Emphasis mine]

The LORD was **sorry.** So sorry, in fact that God went about UNDOING the creation of humans. God did this, not because God planned it that way, but because God regretted the outcome of this act. The LORD saw, that is to say, observed that which

God had not intended, and went about to reverse the unwanted outcome.

The second occasion is in Genesis 22, with the story of Abraham's willingness to sacrifice Isaac. In 22:7ff, we read,

> Isaac said to his father Abraham, Father! And he said, Here I am, my son. He said, The fire and the wood are here, but where is the lamb for a burnt offering? 8Abraham said, God himself will provide the lamb for a burnt offering, my son. So the two of them walked on together. 9When they came to the place that God had shown him, Abraham built an altar there and laid the wood in order. He bound his son Isaac, and laid him on the altar, on top of the wood. 10Then Abraham reached out his hand and took the knife to kill his son. 11 But the angel of the LORD called to him from heaven, and said, Abraham, Abraham! And he said, Here I am. 12He said, Do not lay your hand on the boy or do anything to him; *for now I know that you fear God, since you have not withheld your son, your only son, from me."* [Emphasis mine]

'…for now I know' Were it not for this reality, this truly not knowing if Abraham were indeed the fit subject for the promised covenant, this whole episode is a sham and a merciless torturing of Abraham. But God did not know, and needed to find out. I hope this isn't too unsettling, as our free will depends upon this.

The third incident is in Exodus, Chapter 32, following the incident of the golden calf, which turns out to be the proverbial last straw demolishing God's patience with Israel.

Beginning at verse 7,

> The LORD said to Moses, I have seen this people, how stiff-necked they are. ¹⁰Now let me alone, so that my wrath may burn hot against them and I may consume them; and of you I will make a great nation. ¹¹But Moses implored the LORD his God, and said, O LORD, why does your wrath burn hot against your people, whom you brought out of the land of Egypt with great power and with a mighty hand? ¹²Why should the Egyptians say, It

was with evil intent that he brought them out to kill them in the mountains, and to consume them from the face of the earth? Turn from your fierce wrath; ***change your mind*** and do not bring disaster on your people. [13]Remember Abraham, Isaac, and Israel, your servants, how you swore to them by your own self, saying to them, I will multiply your descendants like the stars of heaven, and all this land that I have promised I will give to your descendants, and they shall inherit it forever. [14]***And the LORD changed his mind*** about the disaster that he planned to bring on his people. [Emphasis mine]

The LORD changed his mind. God was willing to destroy all of Israel, but for Moses, and begin again with him. Were it not for Moses intercession, this story would have had an entirely different outcome. That's taking this story seriously. I think that this is taking it and the other examples of God changing God's mind on their own terms. Think about this: If this were not the case, then prayer is useless. What Moses did is called intercessory prayer. Don't Christians believe that prayer works because God can change outcomes that would have gone otherwise had we not prayed?

I am committed to the notion that what we are living through in our lives isn't some movie that God is watching with the heavenly court that never changes no matter how many times it is replayed. God is indeed watching and wishing to partner with us, and often does, as we live our lives out together, in an open-ended future. That's Genesis!

Consistent with what we have seen in God's actions, God's first experiment to find a suitable helper for the man ended unsuccessfully. It is only after the man turns down every creature presented to him that God created the woman. Verse 23 is very telling here: Then the man said, This at last [after all the foregoing effort] is bone of my bones and flesh of my flesh; this one shall be called Woman, for out of Man this one was taken.

Among the many details of this story, I find three appropriate for this discussion:

1. God's first intention was to limit the initial creation to "the man." The man's loneliness precluded this.
2. God's first choice for a companion to the lonely man was not a woman, it was a creature.
3. No matter what the man's choice was, it was the man's choice. God did not force the woman on the man; the man told God, this, at last, is the one for him.

God trusted the man to make the appropriate choice. The decision was always the man's. God's role here is facilitator to end the man's loneliness, not the dictator of how to fix the man's loneliness.[1]

There is no way that a doctrine of the exclusivity of heterosexuality can be adduced from this story. If anything, the woman, and sex, are afterthoughts, contingencies required of the changing situation. This is consistent with the texts regarding the experimental nature of God with humanity we've already seen (Genesis 6:5-6; Genesis 22:7-12; Exodus 32:7- 14). Perhaps better put, God is willing to adapt to realities that present themselves owing to the nature of free will and its, often, unexpected consequences.

From these realities, I ask these questions:

1. Since heterosexuality is a contingency, why can't nonheterosexuals be considered a contingency?
2. Since God allowed "the man" to make his own choice, why is it not consistent for today's nonheterosexual person to make his or her own choice?

---

1   As an aside, it must be pointed out that this is a highly patriarchal, even misogynist point of view, as the interest of the woman is not of concern here. To make it universal, *ha 'adam* must represent humanity, and therefore the interest of the woman is considered equal to that of the man. The woman is free to choose for herself as the man is for himself. But in biblical days, this was not possible.

3. Since overcoming loneliness is the objective, and since a nonheterosexual's loneliness can't be overcome in a heterosexual relationship, isn't it proper for a nonheterosexual to find a companion suitable for him or her?

So we need to listen carefully to the stories of creation in Genesis. Since heterosexuality is merely a contingency of creation, what can be adduced from Genesis is heterosexuality, expressed as the procreative ability, is the norm, but certainly not the sole sexuality. Yes, the couple is now told to *be fruitful and multiply, and fill the earth and subdue it;* but reproductive capability has never been a mandatory criterion for being a full human being who bears the image of God, or for being married.

So, I thank these authors for pointing out to us that one of the great benefits of marriage is that it enables us to overcome our loneliness. Given that God literally moved heaven and earth to accomplish this, shouldn't this same God-like attitude prevail for all God's children?

Sodom and Gomorrah:
Much ado about homosexual nothing—Genesis 19

One of the things that makes biblical interpretation so thorny is the difficulty of moving from one culture to another. If the Bible is read the same way one reads the newspaper, thinking that things then are just like things now, the first mistake is made and a false outcome is guaranteed. This is especially true with the story of Sodom and Gomorrah.

Let's take a step back before we get into the text and see what cultural norms are operating here. The early second millennium BC was a particularly harsh time for desert dwellers. Travel in these days was complicated by bandits, harsh weather and predatory animals. One literally put one's life in jeopardy when traveling. That's why traveling by caravan was so popular. So to alleviate as much misery as possible, a "hospitality ethic" was born.

The hospitality ethic, practiced throughout the Middle East, was to ensure the safe passage of strangers while they traveled. The way it worked is illustrated in the story just preceding this with the arrival of the strangers to Abraham's encampment. Abraham bows down to the strangers, showing greeting, not hostility; Abraham orders a fine dinner prepared for them, and then personally stands watch over them while they ate, as he was now responsible for their safety. This was not done because people in those days were especially nice to each other, or there was an abundance of food to go around. No. It was to ensure that a city or tribe got a good reputation for hospitality so that its citizens, when traveling, would be accorded the same good treatment. If a city had a bad reputation, its travelers would not find a hospitable welcome away from home.

It is in the context of the hospitality ethic that the story of Sodom and Gomorrah unfolds. Aliens come to the home of a resident alien, Lot. This is grounds for grave suspicion. Could they be planning something against us? The citizens demand to have the strangers brought out so they may "know" *yadha* them.

In the Septuagint, the rabbis translated the Hebrew word *yadha* into a Greek word that can mean "to interrogate" the strangers. The rabbis saw this story as a typical reaction to strangers and the need to know their motives.

It is fairly obvious that the citizens' intention was to rape the strangers. Not "to have sex with them", but to rape them. Lot counters with an offer to allow the men to rape his daughters. (One could digress here and point out that this isn't what any of us would do today. Offering our daughters is not an act of hospitality we would consider appropriate as a host. That's why we can't assume that things then are like things now. Yet, Lot was obliged to make any concession to protect those who came into his home.)

Note: there is nothing consensual in either case, the strangers or the daughters. Male on male rape was a common aspect of ancient Near Eastern society regarding enemies. Rape was (and still is) an effort to humiliate and control. The usual practice after a war victory was to rape the remaining soldiers into submission as a show of dominance. *Ancient Near Eastern museums display artworks depicting this, such as the one on a vase in Figure 2. It depicts a Greek soldier about to rape a defeated and horrified Persian.*

[Figure 2]

This aspect of rape is depicted by the men of Sodom saying, *This fellow [Lot] came here as an alien and he would play the judge! Now we will deal worse with you than with them.* They were going to rape Lot, too!

We now know that rape has nothing to do with sex, except that it is done with the genitals. To say that rape is sex is to say that we kiss a drumstick while our lips assist in tearing meat from the bone. Therefore, this is a story of rape, having nothing to do with sex, let alone, homosexual sex.

This story is concerned about abuse of the stranger, not about homosexuals. The sin here has absolutely nothing to do with homosexuals at all.

Here's the witness of the Bible, itself:

Isaiah 1:10,17

Hear the word of the Lord, you rulers of Sodom! Listen to the teaching of our God, you people of Gomorrah!...Learn to do good; seek justice, rescue the oppressed, defend the orphan, plead for the widow.

Ezekiel 16:48-50 Regarding Jerusalem

As I live, says the Lord God, your sister Sodom and her daughters have not done as you and your daughters have done. [49] This was the guilt of your sister Sodom: she and her daughters had pride, excess of food, and prosperous ease, but did not aid the poor and needy. [50]They were haughty, and did these abominable things before me; therefore I removed them when I saw it.

Zephaniah 2:9-10

Therefore, as I live, says the LORD of hosts the God of Israel,

Moab shall become like Sodom
and the Ammonites like Gomorrah,
a land possessed by nettles and salt pits,
and a waste forever.

The remnant of my people shall plunder them,
and the survivors of my nation shall possess them.

[10] This shall be their lot in return for their pride,
because they scoffed and boasted
against the people of the LORD of hosts.

Book of Wisdom 19:13-18 (Roman Catholic Bible), regarding Sodom and Gomorrah

On the sinners, punishment rained down not without violent thunder as early warning; and deservedly they suffered for their crimes, since they evinced such bitter hatred for strangers.

Church Father, Origen (185-254 C.E.)

"Hear this, you who close your homes to guests! Hear this, you who shun the traveler as an enemy! Lot lived among the Sodomites. We do not read of any other good deeds of his:…He escaped the flames, escaped the fire, on account of one thing only. He opened his home to guests. The angels entered the hospitable household; the flames entered those homes closed to guests." (*Homilia Vin Genesim*)

Leviticus: When is an abomination not an abomination?

Here are the two passages in Leviticus that are at the center of the controversy: (Leviticus 18:22) You shall not lie with a male as with a woman; it is an abomination. And (Leviticus 20:13) If a man lies with a male as with a woman, both of them have committed an abomination; they shall be put to death; their blood is upon them. Quite straightforward, aren't they. After reading this in my seminar, I would close the Bible, and announce that the seminar is over. This is so clear, how could anyone with any credibility believe that God approves of LGBTs after hearing this? Moses wanted them executed; how could this possibly be defended?

One might be excused in believing that this is the last word on the subject who reads the Bible strictly on a "face value" basis. "It says what it means and means what it says." But that is often a very misleading way to read the Bible, as we shall see.

Just what is meant by a biblical abomination? Here are a couple of other interesting abominations in the stories about Joseph.

(Genesis 43:32) *They served him by himself, and them by themselves, because the Egyptians could not eat with the Hebrews, for that is an abomination to the Egyptians.*

(Genesis 46:34) *When Pharaoh calls you, and says, 'What is your occupation?' you shall say, 'Your servants have been keepers of livestock from our youth even until now, both we and our ancestors'—in order that you may settle in the land of Goshen, because all shepherds are abhorrent [toévah] to the Egyptians.*

Some abominations are clearly culturally derived.

Here are some other notable abominations (all from the Hebrew *toévah*).
Observing the nakedness of a relative
Sex during menstruation
Eating shrimp, lobster, rabbit, pork, etc.
Wearing of other gender's clothing
Planting two different crops in the same field
Wearing clothing of two different fabrics
Spots on a priest's bald head
Eating fruit from a tree less than five years old

Abominations, all. So, if you are a woman reading this wearing bluejeans, you are an abomination. If you are anyone wearing a cotton/polyester shirt, you are an abomination. If you are a farmer planting hybrid crops, you are an abomination. If you raise cattle or livestock, all hybrids, you are an abomination. If you had a shrimp cocktail or pork cutlet for dinner last night, you are an abomination.

I think you get the point. However, some miss it entirely, as they know that all these are also biblical abominations which require the trespasser to avoid all such behavior, yet blithely, even cavalierly, think nothing of ignoring these biblical abominations. Yet they insist on holding steadfastly to the one and only one regarding what they think is same-sex lovemaking. (It's not, as discussed below.)

The problem, though, is that this is a package deal. We can't just pick and choose what abominations we will observe and which we will ignore. They all stand or fall together. Some have no problem ignoring the shrimp prohibition or any of the others, except the ONE that bothers them the most. I'll let you decide why this one and only this one is picked as the inviolable one… "because the Bible says so."

But what about the Levitical death penalty?

Yet, this prohibition carries with it capital punishment, as both of them have committed an abomination; they shall be put to death; their blood is upon them. What about it? Shouldn't we place this into a special category? Well, let's see. Here are other Laws that require the death penalty:

> A child cursing one's parents
> A woman's lack of virginity on the wedding night
> Adultery
> Incest
> Working on the Sabbath day

Would those who insist on upholding Leviticus 20:13 insist also on making each of these a capital offense? I think not. So why the ONE?

If we executed every child who cursed its parents, and every person who committed adultery, there would be few adults left to raise the remaining children. (Let alone, serve in Congress.) And as loathsome as incest is, we aren't about to begin killing its perpetrators. So let's cut the hypocrisy here and admit that there are no grounds for insisting on keeping the Levitical prohibition in place.

But there is one more piece of work left to do. I introduced the cultural aspect of how abominations are formed with the examples of Joseph in Egypt. In America, I might ask if you had sautéed poodle for dinner last night? That would appall you, wouldn't it. Other cultures might find it appetizing. It is the culture that creates what is approved or not. In Israel, coming into the Canaanite territory, the temptation was always to adopt the habits and mores of their neighbors. All the prophets railed against this, and Moses stipulated against certain things that would draw the Israelites closer to worshiping Baal. The Lord spoke to Moses, saying: Speak to the people of Israel and say to them: I am the Lord your God. You shall not do as they do in the land of Egypt, where you lived, and you shall not do as they do in the land of Canaan. (Leviticus 18:3)

One example is male temple prostitution.

> (1 Kings 14:24) ...*there were also male temple prostitutes in the land. They committed all the abominations of the nations that the Lord drove out before the people of Israel.*

The Levitical prohibition certainly was aimed at forbidding this abomination and may have been the only reason for it, as nowhere in the Mosaic Law is female to female sex banned.

Who does Paul have in mind in Romans 1?

We need to clear some of the debris out of the way before we can get into the specifics of this most vitriolic of rants by Paul, Romans 1:18-32.

The first observation is that there is no word or combination of words that can be translated "homosexual," or its synonyms, in Greek (or Hebrew, for that matter). Linguists know that without a word there is no concept. So to believe that what we know as homosexuality today existed in the same form 2000 years ago is quite wrong. To use the word homosexual (sodomite, etc.) in an English translation is to put words in apostles' mouths (or in their pens, as it were).

Some translations that use the "Dynamic Equivalent" mode of translation think they found the equivalent in either homosexual or Sodomite, but there is no equivalent extant today. Even the NRSV, a non-Dynamic Equivalent translation, mistranslated the word and has no excuse. So the people who can quote their translation thinking they are quoting the Bible are only misquoting the original.

So, point number one is that whatever it is that Paul is talking about here it is decidedly not homosexuality as we know it today. The Bible can't condemn that which it knows nothing about.

The Greek word for nature, *physis,* as used by Paul, isn't at all what conservative interpreters want it to mean, that is, equivalent to Natural Law, or the way God made things. Quite to the contrary, as seen in Paul's use of the word in 1 Corinthians 11:14, Does not nature itself teach you that if a man wears long hair, it is degrading to him. One is entitled to ask, in what way does nature teach this? Well, it doesn't. Paul came to his belief about the length of hair by way of his culture's teachings which are received as the way things are (or should be!). My mother was roundly condemned by her mother when she "bobbed" her hair (cut it short) as a young woman in the Roaring Twenties. Grandmother was simply put off because she and her peers were taught that short hair on a woman meant she was "loose." Today, short hair is considered inconsequential. Nature has nothing to do with it.

Troy W. Martin, a medical historian, in an article in the Journal of Biblical Literature, tells us how Paul and his contemporaries came to this conclusion about hair.[1] Since the time of Hippocrates to well beyond Paul's day, hair was considered to be a sexual object. The Greek word for hair and testes is the same word. That's why women were to cover their hair, as it was considered erogenous. Hair also had a procreative function. It was thought to be hollow and therefore created a vacuum. This was thought to pull the sperm into the womb. A woman who was not able to conceive had a pungent suppository placed in her vagina and told to return the next day. If the physician could smell the odor in the woman's mouth, she was thought able to conceive; if not, she was considered infertile.

---

1   *Journal of Biblical Literature,* 123/1 (2004)

Naturally (if you'll forgive the pun), it worked the same way in the male. Long hair pulled the man's sperm away from the source making procreation more difficult, if not impossible. Therefore, long hair would be deemed unnatural and degrading to a man. Short hair on a woman was, likewise, degrading (why it was often cut off as punishment). Both were rejecting their "natural" roles as procreators.

So, when Paul appeals to "nature," he is merely reflecting the notions of his (Hellenic/Jewish) culture and not relaying truth fallen from heaven. His information is only as good as his culture can make it. Christians are under no obligation to follow it.

The most despicable people in the world

We can "cut to the chase" very quickly by beginning at the end. To see where Paul is headed is to see what concerns him. And it should concern us, too.

Whoever it is that Paul is castigating here surely are among humanity's most despicable people. Here's how the NRSV puts it:

> They were filled with every kind of wickedness, evil, covetousness, malice. Full of envy, murder, strife, deceit, craftiness, they are gossips, slanderers, God-haters, insolent, haughty, boastful, inventors of evil, rebellious toward parents, foolish, faithless, heartless, ruthless. They know God's decree, that those who practice such things deserve to die—yet they not only do them but even applaud others who practice them.

No one of wholesome spirit would want to be associated in any way with such as these. These are the dregs of the earth, for sure. This is character shaped by idolatry; that is, shaped by other than God.

We begin here because I want you to consider something in your own experience. Do you know any Christian LGBTs who fit this description? Certainly not. They fit, instead, another of Paul's lists of characteristics, the fruit of the Spirit: love, joy, peace, patience, kindness, generosity, faithfulness. If this isn't your experience, you don't know enough gay Christians! Therefore, I can say with assurance that whomever Paul has in mind, it isn't gay Christians!

It must also be said that this does not fit even the vast majority of LGTB people at all. The prejudicial depiction of the stereotypical gay is a product of projecting a minority of gays as typical of the whole. Even in a pride parade, the exhibitionists are in the minority.

I know hundreds of LGBT Christians, many of whom make my witness look puny. I also know gays who have been driven from our churches by behavior more typical of the strife, deceit, craftiness, gossip, slanderer, insolent, haughty, boastful behavior that Paul decries, than that of the Spirit.

Have we misread the Bible?

The history of interpreting this Romans 1 has taken a turn in recent scholarship. One of the most important insights came from asking a simple question: If what we know as sexual orientation (that is, heterosexuality, homosexuality and the like) is a product of modern psychological study, and are foreign concepts in biblical days, have we misread the Bible? Another way of putting the question is, Have we assumed that Paul has these modern categories in mind in Romans 1? If we do not, and I believe we shouldn't or we are invoking anachronisms, then a whole new outcome is revealed, one that can no longer support the view that Paul is denouncing gays and lesbians. How can this be?

Not only did Paul not work with the unknown (to his age) categories of sexual orientation, he did not even think in terms of homosexual behavior, either. Sex for him and his Greco-Roman contemporaries was ethical or unethical, appropriate or inappropriate. Worst of all was sex that was driven by passion.[1]

---

1   For those of you who want to dig deeper into this, a good
     starting place is an article by New Testament scholar, David
     E. Fredrickson, found h e r e: http://books.google.com/
     booksid=6pCEjNJexFYC&printsec=frontcover#v=onepage&f=false and in

A revealing notion from a Greek philosopher, Dio Chrysostom, (a contemporary of Paul) is that he assumed that the same lust that drove a man to seek intercourse with women would lead the same man to intercourse with men.[1] He would think this because sexual orientation was not a category known to him; passion drove sexual desire. Lust, or passion, was considered the most harmful of the influences on one's life. The ideal man (sic) is the one who is virtually passionless, who is always in full control of his emotions.

This is easily seen in the way that Luke (the author of this Gospel is a classically trained Greek) eliminates the emotions from Mark's depictions of Jesus. Here are just a couple of examples.

> (Mark 4:20) *And these are the ones sown on the good soil; they hear the word and accept it and bear fruit, thirty and sixty and a hundredfold.*

> Luke adds the description of the ideal person. (Luke 8:15) *But as for that in the good soil, these are the ones who, when they hear the word, hold it fast in an honest and good heart, and bear fruit with patient endurance.*

> (Mark 3:5) *He looked around at them with anger; he was grieved at their hardness of heart and said to the man, "Stretch out your hand." Luke omits the emotions altogether.*

> (Luke 6:10) *After looking around at all of them, he said to him, "Stretch out your hand." Take out your concordance and see for yourself how many times....*

> Luke disregards Mark's emotional Jesus. His Jesus is the Hellenistic perfect man, virtually devoid of emotion.

With this in mind let's take a closer look at 1:26-27 (NRSV)

So Paul wrote: *For this reason God gave them up to degrading passions. Their women exchanged natural inter-*

---

the book, *Homosexuality, Science, and the Plain Sense of Scripture,* by David L. Balch

1   "The Fourth Discourse on Kingship", v. 120

course for unnatural, and in the same way also the men,
giving up natural intercourse with women, were consumed
with passion for one another. Men committed shameless acts
with men and received in their own persons the due penalty
for their error.

If we don't immediately assume lesbianism at work here in
Their women exchanged natural intercourse for unnatural, it isn't
necessary to import it. It is open to a variety of meanings. And
the expression in the same way also the men means that passion
invaded their bodies just like it invaded the women's bodies. So
the due penalty for their error was indeed received in their own
persons, that is, in their own bodies, that despicable source of all
evil, passion.

When we delve deeply into the prevailing context of the biblical era, we discover an almost impenetrable distance. So different,
in fact, that we end up comparing apples with oranges, or in this
case, equating modern sexual orientation with a Stoic distaste of
emotion and think they are the same thing. They are not. The
notion that two people of the same sex could love each other and
be as committed to one another as any heterosexual couple was
as foreign to him as this idolatry/passion related explanation is to
us. Surely only stubbornness can explain why people continue to
believe our present day LGBTs fit this description. For the source
of their orientations, we must look elsewhere. Romans 1 needs to
be removed from the index of charges against them. Yes, idolatry
has its casualties; let's not add LGBTs to that list.

Is it possible for gays' sexual orientation to be changed to heterosexual?—1 Corinthians 6:9-11

Herman Goebbels was right: tell a lie often enough and soon
it will be thought to be the truth. Such a lie has been circulating for
a few decades now, but is finally being held up to the light of truth,
scientific truth to be exact. It is the lie that gays can be made straight
through proper counseling and prayer. It's been stylized as "Pray

away the gay," in many conservative Christian churches and movements. Exodus International is the leading organization contending that gays can change their orientation. No less an authority than Exodus International president Alan Chambers completely reversed his longstanding view that gays can be made straight. Here's the full quote: "The majority of [gay] people that I have met, and I would say the majority meaning 99.9% of them, have not experienced a change in their orientation." (Interestingly, that would likely include himself, who has for years claimed an orientation change.

I have on a CD, a speech from a former member of Exodus International's board of directors suggesting that, since a preponderance of gays don't change, Exodus International should change its motto from "Change Is Possible through Jesus Christ" to "Come suffer with us." This underscores the plight of their followers who are told that they can't act on their sexuality or risk going to hell. They must resist their temptations, and, yes, they suffer for it. One can't help but admire their commitment, but also grieve at how unnecessary their plight is.

There has been only one "scientific" study that has held that gays do change. It was conducted by none other than the psychologist who led the American Psychological Association to remove homosexuality from the list of mental disorders in 1973, Dr. Robert Spitzer. It was his presumed objectivity that gave the study its prestige. Recently, Dr. Spitzer retracted his study with an apology to the gay community for the harm he had caused.[1]

So, what drives the conservative Christian movement to applaud such studies and accept this lie at face value? Very simply, it's all about one short paragraph in the Bible, 1 Corinthians 6:9-11.

---

1   Here is the text of the written apology: "I believe I owe the gay community an apology for my study making unproven claims of the efficacy of reparative therapy. I also apologize to any gay person who wasted time and energy undergoing some form of reparative therapy because they believed that I had proven that reparative therapy works with some 'highly motivated' individuals. Robert Spitzer. M.D."

Do you not know that wrongdoers will not inherit the kingdom of God? Do not be deceived! Fornicators, idolaters, adulterers, male prostitutes, sodomites, thieves, the greedy, drunkards, revilers, robbers—none of these will inherit the kingdom of God. And **this is what some of you used to be.** But you were washed, you were sanctified, you were justified in the name of the Lord Jesus Christ and in the Spirit of our God. [Emphasis mine]

This verse straightforwardly states that some in the congregation were once sodomites, but are no longer. Sodomites, erroneously, are understood to be today's homosexuals. Many gay Christians took this verse to heart and subjected themselves to every conceivable treatment to rid themselves of this condition because they believed what they read. (Mel White estimates he paid nearly $500,000 in efforts to change his orientation, including shock treatments.) However, this verse does not actually say anything of the kind. The translation, sodomites, was not coined until 1000 years after the Bible was written, so its use here is anachronistic. Therefore, a more suitable translation is required, and one is at hand: users of temple prostitutes. Male prostitutes were temple prostitutes in Corinth and they had customers/users. These are the people under consideration in this paragraph, and no wonder Paul could claim that they were washed, they were sanctified, they were justified in the name of the Lord Jesus Christ....But to expect the same for nonheterosexuals isn't warranted or even possible, and NOT under consideration in this paragraph.

Here's a sampling of what experts in their fields have to say about the impossibility of changing sexual orientation and the harm it causes:

American Academy of Pediatrics (1993)

"Therapy directed specifically at changing sexual orientation is contraindicated, since it can provoke guilt and anxiety while having little or no potential for achieving changes in orientation." American Medical Association (2003)

"Our AMA opposes the use of 'reparative' or 'conversion' therapy that is based on the assumption that homosexuality per se is a mental disorder or based upon the a priori assumption that the patient should change his/her homosexual orientation." American Psychoanalytic Association (2000)

"Psychoanalytic technique does not encompass purposeful efforts to 'convert' or 'repair' an individual's sexual orientation. Such directed efforts are against fundamental principles of psychoanalytic treatment and often result in substantial psychological pain by reinforcing damaging internalized homophobic attitudes."

American Psychiatric Association (1998)

"The American Psychiatric Association opposes any psychiatric treatment, such as reparative or conversion therapy, which is based upon the assumption that homosexuality per se is a mental disorder or based upon the priori assumption that a patient should change his/her sexual homosexual orientation." The APA removed homosexuality from its list of disorders in 1973.

American Psychological Association (1997)

"No scientific evidence exists to support the effectiveness of any of the conversion therapies that try to change sexual orientation." The association removed homosexuality from its list of disorders in 1975.

National Association of Social Workers (2000)

"People seek mental health services for many reasons. Accordingly, it is fair to assert that lesbians and gay men seek therapy for the same reasons that heterosexual people do. However, the increase in media campaigns, often coupled with coercive messages from family and community members, has created an environment in which lesbians and gay men often are pressured to seek reparative or conversion therapies, which cannot and will not change sexual orientation…. Specifically, transformational ministries are fueled by stigmatization of lesbians and gay men, which in turn produces the social climate that pressures some people to seek change in sexual orientation. No data demonstrate that reparative or conversion therapies are effective, and in fact they may be harmful."

Gays can't change their orientation any more than straights can. Since God made each of us in our own special way, why would we want to?

A journey into the heart of God

"The essential problem before the church is not reconciling homosexuality with the Bible, but to reconcile the continuous abuse and condemnation of gay and lesbian persons with the love of Christ."
~ The Reverend Dr. Harold Porter

Entering into the heart of God is the most important journey a Christian can take. If you know the heart of God you know how you are to live. The Bible isn't an answer book for every question that a person may ask. However, principles emerge from it that can orient us in such a way that answers emerge. How can we tell what is in God's heart?

Casual readers of the Bible are quite surprised to learn that the Bible isn't univocal, that is, it does not speak with the same voice and have the same view on all subjects. In fact, the Bible can be said to argue with itself. The writer of Ecclesiastes, for example, has problems with the teachings of Deuteronomy. He knows that Moses taught that the righteous will prosper and the evil will perish, but when he looks around he observes just the opposite. James and Paul differed on the vital question of salvation. Paul taught that saving faith was without works, while James insisted that works were involved. You can't get much farther apart than these two examples demonstrate.

What's the answer? How can we make sense out of the Bible? How can we harvest from the Bible the best that it has to offer and set aside all that would distract us from an ennobling relationship with God and one another? How can we get inside God's heart?

The canon within the Canon

One answer is what theologians call "a canon within the Canon." A canon is a rule. Just as with a ruler, a canon is placed alongside something to measure it. Everyone has a canon within the Canon of the Bible by which to measure the value of any portion of it. Some may protest to the contrary, but it is a universal practice. The differences lay in what a particular person's canon might be. This is admittedly arbitrary as many different choices are available.

Since Jesus is my teacher, I will go with what I see as Jesus' canon within the Canon. Here it is:

> [35]and one of them, a lawyer, asked him a question to test him.[36]"Teacher, which commandment in the law is the greatest?" [37]He said to him, "'You shall love the Lord your God with all your heart, and with all your soul, and with all your mind.' [38]This is the greatest and first commandment. [39]And a second is like it: 'You shall love your neighbor as yourself.' [40]On these two commandments hang all the law and the prophets." (Matthew 22:35-40)

What does it mean to love your neighbor? The problem with this for us as Christians is we are confused about what love means. The difficulty is seen in that even Jesus had a problem communicating its meaning. And what he did was tell the story of the Good Samaritan. The story of the Good Samaritan tells us who our neighbor is, the one who needs us now; this is our neighbor. And this love (*agape'*) isn't butterflies in the stomach. *Agape* love is a very specific kind of love, a love which means whole hearted commitment to the other, to the wellbeing of the other. If you love someone with *agape* love, you love like God loves, with a whole hearted commitment to the wellbeing of the neighbor and the neighbor is that one who needs you now.

Love means caring for the wellbeing of the oppressed

When Jesus says love somebody, that's what he's talking about. He's not saying be nice to people, show them deference. No. Insist on their wellbeing at all times. This is a sacrificial kind of love that goes out of its way to insure that people's needs are being met, that their humanity is kept intact. This he emphasized in his inaugural address at the synagogue in his hometown.

> "The Spirit of the Lord is upon me, because he has anointed me to bring good news to the poor. He has sent me to proclaim release to the captives and recovery of sight to the blind, to let the oppressed go free, to proclaim the year of the Lord's favor." And he rolled up the scroll, gave it back to the attendant, and sat down. The eyes of all in the synagogue were fixed on him. Then he began to say to them, "Today this scripture has been fulfilled in your hearing." (Luke 4:18-21)

Whose side is God on? What Jesus is all about is for the blind to get their sight, the slaves to go free, the poor to receive their sustenance, and the Year of Jubilee (setting things right) is declared.

Jesus is saying, "I am about reversing the oppressive situation in people's lives; that's what I am here for." Jesus undoubtedly got this message of God's love and care for the outcasts by pondering on Israel's story, and noticing the difference between Moses' attitude and God's.

> Moses: *No Ammonite or Moabite shall be admitted to the assembly of the LORD. Even to the tenth generation, none of their descendants shall be admitted to the assembly of the LORD, because they did not meet you with food and water on your journey out of Egypt, and because they hired against you Balaam son of Beor, from Pethor of Mesopotamia, to curse you.*

In other words, these people did not follow the hospitality ethic when Moses and Israel were out in the desert dying of thirst. Therefore, no Moabites, no Ammonites were allowed to go to church with Israel. That is presumably the voice of Moses because he is angry at these nations.

But, Jesus also knew the story of Naomi and Ruth:

> *In the days when the judges ruled, there was a famine in the land, and a certain man of Bethlehem in Judah went to live in the country of Moab, he and his wife and two sons. The name of the man was Elimelech and the name of his wife Naomi, and the names of his two sons were Mahlon and Chilion; they were Ephrathites from Bethlehem in Judah. They went into the country of Moab and remained there. But Elimelech, the husband of Naomi, died, and she was left with her two sons. These took Moabite wives; the name of the one was Orpah and the name of the other Ruth.*

So this is Ruth, a Moabite woman who has a Bible book named after her.

That's not all:

> *So Boaz took Ruth (Boaz is an Israelite) and she became his wife. When they came together, the LORD made her conceive, and she bore a son. The women of the neighborhood gave him a name, saying, "A son has been born to Naomi." They named him Obed; he became the father of Jesse, the father of David.*

The father of King David has Moabite blood in him. The most revered king of Israel was part Moabite, even though Moses condemned them from ever having anything to do with the cult of Israel. But God took care of that in a big way: Jesus was born with Moabite blood, too.

Moses had other prejudices. For instance, eunuchs.

> No one whose testicles are crushed or whose penis is cut
> off shall be admitted to the assembly of the LORD.

If you're a eunuch you can't go to church with Moses. But,
Isaiah, speaking for God a few generations after Moses, says,

> Do not let the foreigner joined to the LORD say, "The
> LORD will surely separate me from his people"; and do not
> let the eunuch say, "I am just a dry tree." For thus says the
> LORD: To the eunuchs who keep my Sabbaths, who choose
> the things that please me and hold fast my covenant, will give,
> in my house and within my walls, a monument and a name
> better than sons and daughters; I will give them an everlasting
> name that shall not be cut off.

We humans have many ways to ostracize people we don't want
around us. God has even more ways to be inclusive, and Jesus
learned these lessons.

The most interesting thing about this whole notion of the un-
acceptability of eunuchs is that the very first Christian convert that
was not an ethnic Jew was an Ethiopian *eunuch,* as told in Acts 8.
When Phillip caught up to him on the chariot he is reading Isaiah.
He's reading out of the very book where he knows he's unwelcome.
At some point in the conversation he stops the chariot and asks,
"Phillip, can I be baptized? What hinders me? The fact that I am
cut off, does that hinder me from being baptized?"

The next verse says that Phillip and the eunuch went down
into the water and Phillip baptized him. The formerly "cut off"
one is now joined to the people of God. God's sanctuary is for all
people.

Not too much farther into the Book of Acts, we are introduced to the most critical decision the apostles had to make: Should
Gentiles be allowed in the church without first becoming Jews and
being circumcised?

In Chapter 10, we are informed about a vision Peter had while he was pondering this issue. This story begins, Meanwhile he stayed in Joppa for some time with a certain Simon, a tanner. The ironic thing about this is tanners were the lowest of the low in Israel. They were perpetually unclean. They worked their animal skins with dog dung and were surrounded by animals' bodily fluids. Consequently, they seldom were seen near the temple, because touching an unclean person rendered the toucher unclean.

So, where does Peter ponder this most vexing question? Not accidentally in this person's home filled with uric acid and all kinds of miserable, unclean things.

So, a messenger from heaven comes to Peter.

> Peter went up on the roof to pray. He became hungry and wanted something to eat; and while it was being prepared, he fell into a trance. He saw the heaven opened and something like a large sheet coming down, being lowered to the ground by its four corners. In it were all kinds of four-footed creatures and reptiles and birds of the air. Then he heard a voice saying, "Get up, Peter; kill and eat." But Peter said, "By no means, Lord; for I have never eaten anything that is profane or unclean." The voice said to him again, a second time, "What God has made clean, you must not call profane."

The messenger says to Peter, "Peter see all the pigs and lobster and everything in there you're not supposed to eat?" "Yeah, I see that." "I want you to kill it and fix it for dinner. I want you to eat these unclean things." Peter says, "I can't do that. My Bible says I can't do that." And the messenger from heaven says, "Regardless, eat it!"

The next thing you know, Peter is with a group of people who are conferring with each other on what to do with the Gentiles. Cornelius. a Gentile, arrives and explains that he has had an experience with God and the Holy Spirit. Peter said, "This must be the explanation of what that vision was about. God is saying we've changed. We are to accept the Gentiles. They are as worthy as anybody to be a part of our lives."

This is just one more example of how God works to bring people together who seem wholly incompatible but are all God's children.

The point of the golden rule

Christians believe that the ultimate picture of what God is like is revealed in Jesus Christ. So, what was in Jesus' heart? *"In everything do to others as you would have them do to you; for this is the law and the prophets."* Of course we know this to be the Golden Rule. It is also a good candidate for a canon within the Canon. Up against Leviticus, it will overcome death every time.

In Jesus day there were negative versions of it floating around. "Don't do to others what you don't want done to you. Don't do that. Don't be a part of the problem. Don't do that." Jesus said that's not good enough. No. *Do* unto others, be proactive, go out there and begin doing the right thing. Don't just refrain from doing the wrong thing, be proactive and do the right thing. That's what Jesus says the whole Bible teaches. Those who have learned this lesson are working with God to bring to an end all those things that dehumanize and keep people apart.

Jesus and the Sabbath

The Sabbath law was the most sacrosanct law of Israel. It literally defined the faithful Jew. The rabbis had a notion that on that day that every Jew kept the Sabbath perfectly the Messiah would come. So they centered their entire religious experience around the Sabbath. If in Biblical times you were found working on the Sabbath, which included wearing a hat, lifting it up and putting it on your head, you worked and therefore violated the Sabbath. So you can imagine that it was very hard to keep the Sabbath, yet they managed to do it. They stayed home, they didn't do anything. They had ways around it, but that's another story. The Law required stoning for those who broke the Sabbath.

Here's Mark's account of how Jesus handled Sabbath issues:

> *One Sabbath he was going through the grainfields; and as they made their way his disciples began to pluck heads of grain. The Pharisees said to him, "Look, why are they doing what is not lawful on the Sabbath?" And he said to them, "Have you never read what David did when he and his companions were hungry and in need of food? He entered the house of God, when Abiathar was high priest, and ate the bread of the Presence, which it is not lawful for any but the priests to eat, and he gave some to his companions." Then he said to them, "**The Sabbath was made for humankind, and not humankind for the Sabbath.**"* (Mark 2:23-27) [Emphasis mine.]

What Jesus is saying here is any law, *any law that diminishes the humanity of another person should not be obeyed, even if it is the Sabbath law. It doesn't matter what the Bible says.*[1]

Any law, if it's in the Torah, if it's the Sabbath law, or church canon law, if it becomes the enemy of a human being, Jesus teaches us not to honor that law. Are there laws on the books of the churches that dishonor human beings? They are not to be obeyed. The authority of Jesus is behind this. He knew God's heart.

Abraham Lincoln famously said, "Sir, my concern is not whether God is on our side; my greatest concern is to be on God's side, for God is always right." To be on God's side is to be with those who uphold the dignity of all people, regardless of the law.

---

1   It should be noted that Jesus may well be offering a corrective to a misinterpretation of Sabbath law procedure and is actually upholding the Sabbath as long as its interpretations uphold human need and dignity. Therefore, Jesus and his disciples are actually keeping the Sabbath day holy.

Chapter 7 Discussion Starters

1. Did any of these explanations of Bible passages clarify anything for you? If so, what?

2. Describe the lenses people wear when receiving information?

3. How do our lenses differ depending on who we are?

4. Knowing that we all see things differently, how can this make it easier to accept differences?

5. What is the result when people think they read the Bible objectively (without lenses)?

6. What Bible passages influenced your views of homosexuality?

7. Do you have a "canon within the Canon?" If so, what is yours?

8. How does the depiction of God changing God's mind affect your belief in God?

9. Why do you think people freely eat shrimp and work on the Sabbath, but condemn same-sex love?

8

THE GIFTS GAYS BRING

It is our very woundedness, the fractures that we car-
ry as a separate people in a hostile and condemning
world, that make us pervious to God's spirit, open
to the shattering and healing life of God in Christ.
Life has not given us security enough to rest in the
cocoon of custom or inherited beliefs; we are more
vulnerable, both to the worst the world can do to
us and to the best that God can cause to happen in
us. In a sense, we [gays] are the doorways through
which God can enter a society, a church, grown deaf
to God's good news.
~ M.R. Ritley, *Gifted by Otherness*

I write from the perspective of a straight, white, American
male. One reason that some straight, white, American Christians
have difficulty with the notion that gays can contribute to the
well-being of anyone like them is that they see themselves on the
top of the hierarchy of God's elect. *They* are the arbiters and bestow-
ers of gifts, not the recipients. Add to that their inherited "rugged
individualism," where the idea is denigrated that a person should
be in need of anything, and they become reluctant to receive help,
especially from a lesser being. If you can't make it on your own,
you are a failed citizen.

This is a far cry from how the early church, as witnessed to in the New Testament, conducted itself. Theirs was a community where "all things were held in common," where a congregation was greater than the sum of its parts, when the parts were the various spiritual and material gifts individuals shared with each other as they ministered to one another. Paul sums up this ethic in this way:

> *God has so arranged the body, giving the greater honor to the inferior member, that there may be no dissension within the body, but the members may have the same care for one another. If one member suffers, all suffer together with it; if one member is honored, all rejoice together with it.* (1 Corinthians 12:24-25)

This "body," of course, is the congregation. The farther away we move from this ideal, the greater is the difficulty of seeing ourselves as either contributors or recipients of the grace of God as delivered by mortals.

Whenever the church becomes powerful or wealthy, it tends to see itself less in need of God. The apostle Peter came across a cripple who begged him for alms. Peter replied, "Silver and gold have I none, but this I freely give to thee; rise up and walk!" (KJV) Thomas Aquinas once visited the pope's counting house where he discovered the pope sitting at a table covered with gold and silver coins. "Look," said the pope, "Peter no longer needs to say, "Silver and gold have I none." "Yes," replied Thomas. "And neither can he say, 'Rise up and walk!'"

It's a peculiarly American fiction, a myth really, that makes us believe that we can, perhaps even must, make it on our own. No one has or ever will; we are all beholden to a rich infrastructure of influences and support that precede us here and make our way possible. Not until we recover the early church's understanding of mutual aid and support will we ever be able to help the world, much less ourselves, rise up and walk. Nor will we be able to appreciate our need for the gifts gays bring to the church.

The prophet Samuel noticed of God, You deliver a humble people, but your eyes are upon the haughty to bring them down, and it's still the case. Isn't it haughty to refuse to believe that one stands in need of another? And even haughtier still to look down upon other's offers simply because they are different? If you were subject to any of this before you sat down to read this book, I hope that the foregoing has opened up other possibilities for you. Because the church is a place for people to be enriched by the gifts that everyone has and everyone brings to bear on the lives of others. This includes all whom God brings together, regardless of station, race, class, gender, sexual orientation, or any other way that humans find to separate themselves from one another.

Therefore, Paul writes,

> *There is no longer Jew or Greek, there is no longer slave or free, there is no longer male and female;*[1] *for all of you are one in Christ Jesus.* (Galatians 3:28)

The idea that, if you were a Jew, that Greeks (gentiles) had any value; that, if you were a man, a woman could be your equal; that, if you were a free man, a slave was your equal, were all lunacy in that world. Yet the love that Jesus proclaimed on behalf of God was received as just this notion of equality of all, not only in the eyes of God, but in each other's eyes. Back then, "We all stand on level ground at the foot of the cross," was believed and lived out daily.

It's worth pausing to underscore just how revolutionary this equality was. Egalitarianism was unheard of in the Roman Empire, and was not practiced by any of its religions or upheld by any of its philosophers, except perhaps the Cynics, but they were more anarchic than egalitarian. The phrase, "male and female," harkens back to Genesis 1 where God made them, "male and female." Here Paul is undoing the unequal patriarchal roles that characterized "male and female" that no longer obtain in the new order. Now *that* is revolutionary.

Perhaps, now, the church is ready to hear something new. Perhaps, now, the church is open to the possibility that gay broth-

---

1   Even though God "created them male and female," as to gender, Paul erases any distinctions based on patriarchal role models as having value in the Kingdom. Women and men are equal in all respects.

ers and sisters have something to contribute to the wellbeing of congregations. After I have laid out my suggestions as to what that would look like, they should be obvious, not needing either my approval or yours. They are simply self-evident truths. They are gifts I have received myself, and witnessed being bestowed on a sometimes startled, yet ultimately grateful church. They are the very definition of blessing. This list is surely not comprehensive and will be expanded and deepened by many others whose experiences give further testimony to the vitality of and need for the presence of gays in our lives and churches.

The stark reality of oppression in our midst

We are all shocked when we read reports of oppression, or see it on TV, or right before our eyes. The water hosing of blacks in the Deep South during the Civil Rights struggle of the 1950s and '60s brought America's outrage to a level that would never recede and turned the movement into a success. Documentaries that disclose the awful consequences of the kidnapping and selling of young women and girls into prostitution grip our hearts. Scenes of sweatshops and child labor turned Walmart shoppers away from their stores. Immigrant exploitation, especially in farm labor, brought unions into existence. Yet, were it not for our TVs and newspapers, we are often far removed from these realities. Churches are too often islands of insulation from such realities.

Yet, the occasional presence of gays in our congregations is a stark reminder that oppression exists. Unless a congregation is designated as Open and Affirming of LGBTs (or any of the other denominational terms for full acceptance) their members may never have seen gay gifts at work. In most churches today, gays are removed to the margins of congregational life. They are not allowed to preach, teach or help govern. They aren't invited to sit on a committee and are shunned from "helping out" in other ways. They are gossiped about, feared, not considered suitable to be with children, and generally ignored if not snubbed.

One of the suggestions made to congregations that are openly exploring the issue of gay equality is to invite one or more LGBTs in for a conversation where the congregation can hear their stories, ask questions and discover "what they are like." Very seldom is this seen as unseemly or condescending. Imagine if the topic were, "Should we consider African Americans as equal to white Americans?", for this is exactly the situation. Even the closeted racists in the congregation would not dare utter a word of approval for such a forum.

I have been asked to lead such discussions. When I have, my introduction was simply to call attention to this outrageous form of oppression happening right in their midst. Believe me when I say that this caused much more conversation than anything else that came after. When people are first introduced to the reality that even they participate in unseemly things, things that demean and cause harm, change is afoot. Oppression observed often leads to oppression removed.

What oppression, exactly? In addition to the above, in many churches, gays are constantly reminded that they are not welcome by pulpit pronouncements of condemnation ("Gays are in jeopardy of hell unless they repent and give up their evil ways."). Many congregations openly support local and national efforts to restrict their rights, California's Proposition 8 and DOMA, are recent examples. One congregation I know of sponsored a "Let's have dinner tonight at Chic-fil-A" event after that company announced its opposition to same-sex marriage. Ministries are organized around so-called "ex-gay" treatments that attempt to get gays to "pray away the gay."

Even if the congregation is totally open and affirming of non-heterosexuals, they are witnesses to how their beloved members are treated outside their church doors, and they not only weep for them, but mobilize to assist in overcoming societal oppression. Just the mere presence of LGBTs in a congregation is either a reminder of how ill-treated they can be or how much work is yet to be done. Either way, gay presence points to gay oppression.

The stupefying realization that we are oppressors calls us to a remedy: repentance

The classic and still fruitful definition of repentance is "to turn around and go the other way." It's based on the literal definition of the Greek word, *metanoia*. If one finds one's self heading in the wrong direction, like say, the Prodigal Son, who "came to himself," the stark realization that this way leads only to more unwanted results leads us to start heading in the opposite direction, and quickly. Only the most inured can live in a situation that is suffocating to others. Most will either seek remedies or move on. The Christian remedy for participation in oppression is to repent, to turn around and go the other way.

For the Prodigal Son (Luke 15) it meant returning home with the intention of being a servant to the very ones he rejected, including his own family. It's not enough just to say, "I'm sorry," or to have pangs of conscience without change in behavior. For without such change words are hollow and unproductive, both for the oppressor and for the oppressed.

If you recognize yourself in any of the foregoing examples of how heterosexism does its damage, you may be the leaven for the congregation that "leavens the whole lump." If all you can do is to serve as a good example, you will be doing much. It all starts with the resolve to no longer stand by in the presence of spiritual violence, but to actively pursue that which contributes to everyone's wellbeing. That's *metanoia*.

The willingness to love and keep on loving no matter what the cost

When President Obama connected the long line of resistance to oppression "from Seneca Falls, and Selma, and Stonewall," in his Second Inaugural Address, many were unfamiliar with Stonewall. It rightfully belongs in that trinity of milestones along the way to freedom. For Seneca Falls, NY, was the site of the very first women's rights convention in the Western world in 1848. Selma, AL, was the staging area for Martin Luther King's march to Montgomery in 1965 that proved to be the high-water mark for the Civil Rights Movement. And the Stonewall Inn was a bar in Manhattan frequented by drag queens and assorted gay outcasts who were constantly harassed by local police. On June 28, 1969, the police raided Stonewall and for the first time met resistance which lasted over two days. Their defiance of police brutality energized the gay community like nothing before it and the big push for gay rights began in earnest. By the next year, Gay Pride parades were happening all over the large cities and there was no stopping it.

You don't have to die to be a martyr. All you need is the willingness to be one if necessary. All that's needed is the willingness to put one's life, fortune, and sacred honor on the line, risking it all for the sake of justice. It happens in the USA every day by gays and straights alike who are unwilling to sit idly by and suffer in silence.

Soulforce "was founded as an organization with the purpose of nonviolent resistance of oppression of LGBTQ people by religious fundamentalists."[1] During their fifteen years of activism, they have conducted many actions, been arrested and jailed, and stood with the victims of gay oppression, "to stop the violence of [antigay] words, policies, and actions by showing the human face of the suffering they have caused." I stood with them on several occasions and witnessed heavy trucks running us off public sidewalks, angry people spitting in our faces, rocks thrown at us, all the while threats of violence were sounding in our ears. Many of these LGBTs return home to their local congregations where they remain unwelcome, yet sit in silent protest, calling all who observe their loving, nonviolent presence into self-reflection and often to repentance.

One gay man I know attended the same unwelcoming church for years. He's so kind and gentle that they couldn't bring themselves to ask him to leave. He was there every Sunday, attended adult Bible study and many of the governing meetings. Yet they continued their oppressive ways in his presence. His only public statement, and not that often, was, "Just remember, you are talking

---

1   www.soulforce.org

about me." He told me that he rarely needed to repeat it, as his presence was enough of a reminder.

Many other examples don't end as nicely. Many LGBTs have been beaten up and even murdered because they refused to compromise their beliefs in the face of violent hostility. Or, as in the cases of Matthew Shepard and Carl Arthur Warren, murdered simply for being gay.

The thing to consider, if you observe LGBTs in a hostile church, is that they are not there because they want to cause trouble; they are not there because they want justice for themselves and their gay brothers and sisters. No. They are there because they love you. They love you so much they are willing to put up with years of abuse and condemnation. They are there because they want nothing more for you than to recognize your own self-destruction as you continue to abuse other fellow human beings. They are there to help you understand that we are all connected and that injury to another is injury to one's self. They are there to help us all live out the two Great Commandments of God: to love God with all our soul, strength and mind and our neighbor as ourselves. That shouldn't be remarkable; it is the calling of every Christian. But it is remarkable because it is so seldom seen. This is a gift straight Christians refuse at their own peril.

A model of vulnerability

Our congregations are filled with people who feel unaccepted for a variety of reasons that have nothing to do with being gay. Some are alcoholics, or drug users, or victims of spousal abuse. Others are unemployed or underemployed and feel downtrodden. Still others are living lives of quiet desperation for reasons never discussed. Most, if not all of these people are closeted; we seldom get to know their true situations because they are ashamed and feel that if we did know we would surely find them all the more unacceptable.

In every congregation there are people who either don't take communion or who do so feeling they really aren't acceptable in God's eyes, and surely wouldn't be in others' if they only knew them well. In a sermon, I once suggested to a congregation that I wished we were all in Alcoholics Anonymous. People in AA all know they are broken and are about fixing it. With the masks we wear, we hide our brokenness, which is surely a part of everyone, and hope that no one will ever find out. As long as we live this way we will never be made whole.

LGBTs who are falsely accused of unacceptability on the basis of their "otherness" know only too well the reality of exclusion. Yet, there they are, witnessing to the reality of the grace of God at work in their lives. In the words of Bill Countryman,

> We who are lesbian or gay know where the problem lies; we can name it or describe it. And therefore we have something that's a little easier to recognize. That can make our experience a helpful model, a kind of key that can unlock other people's experiences where it hasn't been clear, where a vaguer feeling of being unacceptable, of not being quite right, where not being full members of the family have dogged people.[1]

On one level or another, we are all Prodigal Sons or Daughters. Only those of us who face up to it are truly free and rid of the anxiety of unacceptability. LGBTs are showing the way.

The wholeness of being sexual/spiritual men and women

When's the last time you heard a sermon on sex? I mean the kind that connects sexuality with spirituality, not the kind that condemns fornication and adultery? Probably never. We Americans are still suffering from the Victorian notion of sex as a taboo subject for polite company. Add to that the not so subtle (and wrong-headed) biblical interpretation of the shame of the body at the expense of the spirit. I think most people would rather hear a sermon on why

---

1   William Countryman and M. R. Ritley, *The Gift of Otherness*, p. 60

we need to give more money than why being spiritual means we are also sexual beings. But the presence of LGBTs in congregations forces the acknowledgement that sex is present, and can lead to serious consideration of the role sex plays, not only in one's private life, but in one's spiritual development, as well.

Our gay brothers and sisters are unashamed of the role sex plays in their lives. Interestingly, it is not any more of a role that is in anyone else's life either. Mel White recalls, "When I was on Larry King Live, somebody called in and said, 'What do you guys do in bed?' Larry hung up on him and said, 'that's none of your business.' And I said, 'We've been together in the same bed for 24 years – we're like everybody else, we sleep in bed. And King said: 'Once they find out you're as boring as we are, it's all over.'"

Sex for LGBTs is no more or no less of importance than for anyone else; it just seems like more because they are defined these days by their sexuality and the rest aren't. So their presence invites consideration of how being sexual beings works in the totality of the life of faith.

The reevaluation of family values

At first blush, the reevaluating of family values might not seem like such a good thing. But it doesn't take a genius to note that the family in America is a failing, if not failed, institution. With divorce at near the 50% rate, we all know of single parent families and the struggle to survive that follows. Our poorer neighborhoods are filled with people struggling just to eke out a living, and their children turn to gangs and crime out of a desperate attempt to find sustenance and acceptance. And our more affluent communities don't seem to fare much better in keeping families together or children from drugs and alcohol related activities.

Some of the blame can be laid at the feet of the notion of romantic love. This is the idea that humans "fall in love." You know, it's magic. It just happens. We have no control over it. When, in actuality, we fall in lust and confuse it with love. Not being schooled in the process involved in the ritual of human paring, we are susceptible to this myth. The danger here is that we also succumb to the notion that we also "fall out of love." You know, it's nobody's fault. We're just not in love anymore. It happens. We therefore feel entitled to move on.

The decline of the family in America can be traced from the end of the 19th century when we began to move from being primarily an agricultural nation living on farms and nearby rural towns to being primarily city dwellers. This took us away from three generations living in close proximity to one another which provided great family stability. Families on farms needed to stay together for survival. Children were needed to work the farm and wives were needed to provide the children and keep the house. It was not uncommon for people to marry for convenience and then learn to love each other. In a college class on Marriage and the Family, our professor noted that the 50% divorce rate is actually much lower than we should expect since there is no longer any reason for people to stay together beyond wanting to.

The reaction to all this change came in the rise of organizations in defense of the "traditional family and traditional family values." However, they chose to defend, not the traditional family, but a recent arrival on the American scene, the "nuclear family." Here the family is reduced to mom, dad and the kids, and the values assumed are as taught in religiously conservative churches. The Republican Party endorsed this view of the nuclear family in its 1994 platform and included support for the traditional role for women in the family, opposition to abortion, abstinence education for youth, and opposition to same-sex marriage.

So, what's wrong with defending the family? Well, let's see. Take King Ahab's family. His wife was Jezebel. Now Jezebel worshiped Baal and was responsible for the killing of hundreds of prophets of the God of Israel. She even coveted a vineyard and had the owner stoned to death that she might possess it. Want to defend this family? I doubt it. How about the family of former

House Speaker Newt Gingrich? Now you will have to pick among his three families, so maybe that's not fair.

So perhaps we need to stipulate that we are not obligated to defend any *particular* family, just the generic notion of family. Or better put, we should be defending the *ideal* family and working toward the implementation of it. The problem with this is it assumes that there is such a thing as an ideal family construction, and that it is attainable. There isn't and it isn't.

The belief in the priority of the family as the highest form of human association is based on the assumption of inherent worth. To be sure, families can and do offer many things of value to their members and to society. But overall, families run the gamut of worthwhile to worthless. Beginning with Adam and Eve, biblical families are full of intrigue, incest, rivalries, conspiracies, even murder, as well as genuine affection and care.

People in Jesus' day were identified primarily thorough their family affiliation. Whatever family you were born into determined your destiny. Rulers came from ruling families, priests from priestly families, artisans from artisan families, and slaves from slave families. There was no upward mobility. Upon birth your life was immediately and totally proscribed, your boundaries set. Your father controlled all aspects of your life including whom you would marry. If you were a woman you were at the mercy of your father until married and of your husband thereafter.

The foundation upholding this myth of the "traditional family," is the presumption that it's the one in the Bible and the one Jesus recommends. All you have to do is review Jesus' attitude toward the family and see that it is no more sacrosanct than his view of marriage. One such example is from Mark 3:31-35:

> *Then his mother and his brothers came; and standing outside, they sent to him and called him. A crowd was sitting around him; and they said to him, "Your mother and your brothers and sisters are outside, asking for you." And he replied,* **"Who are my mother and my brothers?" And looking at those who sat around him, he said, "Here are my mother and my brothers!**

Whoever does the will of God is my brother and sister and mother." [Emphasis mine]

Another is found in Mark 10:28-31 where Peter is trying to impress Jesus with how much he and the disciples have sacrificed to follow him:

> *Peter began to say to him, "Look, we have left everything and followed you." Jesus said, "Truly I tell you, there is no one who has left house or brothers or sisters or mother or father or children or fields, for my sake and for the sake of the good news, who will not receive a hundredfold now in this age—houses, brothers and sisters, mothers and children, and fields with persecutions—and in the age to come eternal life. But many who are first will be last, and the last will be first."*

One of Jesus' most controversial demands can only be understood in the light of his insistence on an egalitarian Kingdom of God. *Whoever comes to me and does not hate father and mother, wife and children, brothers and sisters, yes, and even life itself, cannot be my disciple.* (Luke 14:26). The issue is not the despising of mother and father as human beings, but the roles they played in contemporary Palestinian life that put families at odds with Kingdom demands. Jesus' new family was a family of choice bound together, not by patriarchal or any other societal notion of the ideal family, but by radical equality, and living for the wellbeing of one another and serving each other to that end. Jesus' purpose is not to instruct his followers to renounce their relatives, but to reject family notions built around blood, power structures and patriarchal subordination. They would be welcomed into Jesus's new family with a new understanding of roles and relationships.

So it turns out that those who are affirming the nuclear family and its values are trying to maintain a system that seems more like a form of patriarchy where men continue to hold the most power, women are urged to stay at home to raise children, and children are often expected to fulfill the dreams of their parents.

It is true that the later epistles attributed to Paul contain household lists that seem to contradict Jesus' model of family organization. This is accounted for in recent scholarship by noting that these epistles are not from Paul, but from certain successors writing in his name (tradition) who wanted "to make Christianity and Rome safe for one another."[1] This is not the first time Christianity has adapted to its surrounding culture; history is replete with such examples.

It also turns out that gay Christians are modeling just the kind of nontraditional family Jesus had in mind. For gay families are first and foremost families of choice. They are not formed by societal convention but in opposition to it. They are egalitarian through and through and aren't subject to preset expectations for how heads of households are supposed to act because there are none.

People who get to know gay families discover that they are often asked how they are able to run a household without the typical expectations for division of labor, "who's the boss," and how decisions are made. Why these questions? Because people in traditional families want to break out of the often stultifying restrictions imposed on them in traditional families. So the presence of gay families in congregations is a gift that opens up new and freeing possibilities of new life for all families.

---

1   John D. Crossan, and Jonathan L. Reed. *In Search of Paul, p. 106*

Chapter 8 Discussion Starters

1. How is a congregation affected when it overlooks or refuses to use all the gifts of its members?

2. Of the many gifts gays bring to a congregation, how many are missing in your church?

3. Which gifts would be most beneficial at this time?

4. Which gifts are presently observable from gay members?

5. Why is it hard to be served, or to receive gifts, especially from gay members?

6. Why is putting too much emphasis on the family possibly harmful to the church?

7. What aspects of patriarchalism are left over in our families today? How can we get closer to Jesus' view of the family?

AFTER THE SUPREME COURT DECISION: WHERE TO GO FROM HERE?

*If moral disapprobation of homosexual conduct is
"no legitimate state interest" for purposes of proscrib-
ing that conduct…what justification could there
possibly be for denying the benefits of marriage to
homosexual couples exercising 'the liberty protected
by the Constitution?*
~ Justice Antonin Scalia[1]

First, America needs a civics lesson

Contrary to the National Organization for Marriage's wishes and all others who were disappointed when California's Proposition 8 was struck down, and feel abused, the people DO NOT get to decide what's constitutional and what's not. Fortunately, we live in a constitutional republic, not a pure democracy. For in a pure democracy, if 51% of the people want to cut off the heads of the other 49%, for whatever reason, it would happen. Our Constitution forbids majority coercion of the minority and in fact was created, in no small part, to protect the rights of the minority. So if, say, California passes a proposition that provides that "only marriage

---

1   This quote is taken from his minority dissent to *Lawrence v. Texas when
the court struck down sodomy laws.*

between a man and a woman is valid or recognized in California," the fact that the majority of voters voted yes does not mean it passes constitutional muster. The same holds true for DOMA. That's why, for those who are opposed to marriage equality, DOMA is not enough and only a Constitutional amendment will do.

Ironically, if we were to let the people decide, as NOM would have it, the tide has turned and the majority of Californians and Americans are now in favor of same-sex marriage. Given their favorable attitude toward LGBTs, when the Millennial generation assumes power, this will be a long forgotten era of American history. Just as today when young people are told of Jim Crow and the struggle for Civil Rights, and they are mystified as how this could ever have been, so too will generations from now find it hard to believe that gay people couldn't get married.

How DOMA and Prop 9 control the lives of LGBTs up to now

The federal Defense of Marriage Act effectively does two things. First, it defines marriage for federal purposes as between one man and one woman as husband and wife; and "spouse" refers only to a person of the opposite sex who is either husband or wife. Second, it allows states the right to decline to recognize same-sex marriages that are legal in other states.

The federal General Accounting Office identified "1,049 federal statutory provisions classified to the United States Code in which benefits, rights, and privileges are contingent on marital status or in which marital status is a factor".[1] This shuts out LGBTs from all federal benefits accorded to opposite-sex couples, including income tax breaks, Social Security survivor's benefits, and health care. The GAO upgraded the number of benefits to 1,139 in 2003.

In California, Proposition 8 is a constitutional amendment, passed in 2008, which said marriage defined as "only between a man and a woman is valid or recognized in California." It overturned the

---

1   General Accounting Office. January 31, 1997

California Supreme Court's ruling that banning same-sex marriage is unconstitutional. There was a window from June 16 to November 5, 2009 when same-sex marriage was legal and these marriages continue to be legal and likely will not be affected by SCOTUS's ruling.

The challenge to the constitutionality of both DOMA (*U.S. v. Windsor*) and Prop 8 *(Perry v. Brown)* are currently before the U.S. Supreme Court.

Possible Supreme Court outcomes

Most court watchers count the possible outcomes as four or five, reducing the likely outcomes to three. They range in scope from total victory for marriage equality across the board, to the status quo remaining in place. We will look at each outcome from best to worst, at least in the eyes of supporters of same-sex marriage.

DOMA and Proposition 8 are both struck down

Marriage would become the legal right of every couple, regardless of sexual orientation. Although this is the least likely outcome, it is possible. It is, of course, the most desirable outcome for those of us working for marriage equality. The reality that no couple in America could be denied the full dignity and rights presently accorded only to opposite-sex couples would mean that LGBTs are no longer second-class citizens.

A narrow interpretation would restore same-sex marriage rights to California and confer federal marriage benefits to all legally married same-sex couples throughout America. It would not affect marriage bans in other states; they would remain intact.

DOMA struck down, but Prop 8 upheld

Legally married same-sex couples in California and elsewhere will begin receiving the 1,139 federal marriage benefits. However, same-sex marriage will not be legal in California as well as the other states with similar bans. Those Californians legally married in 2009 will most likely not have their marriages made null and void.

Prop 8 struck down, but DOMA upheld

With the demise of Prop 8, marriage equality will be reinstated in California, and may overturn similar bans in place in other states. However, legally married same-sex couples will be denied all federal rights and benefits related to marriage. Second-class citizenship will continue.

Where do we go from here?

Should SCOTUS grant a sweeping revamping of marriage entitlements that places all couples in America on the same level, our first reaction as recipients and allies should be to celebrate with humility. Yes, we should gather in our local communities, places of worship, and homes with friends and neighbors, to celebrate that the stated intention of our Founders, that "all men [and women] are created equal," is now a reality. We achieved this, not through armed uprising, but by vigorous, relentless voicing of this indignity and revealing to the world that ours is a just cause. We have every right to rejoice in our good fortune.

We also need to remember that others will be devastated. Even though some in the opposition lied, cheated and bullied their way through the contentious decades of this struggle, many hold to such opposition out of sincerely held beliefs. All we have to do is recall our own feelings when things didn't go our way to understand how others may feel. This demonstrates what we have been saying all along: we share a common humanity. Gloating is reserved for those who don't appreciate this.

Should we receive a narrower victory, with DOMA and Prop 8 gone, yet with marriage bans still in place outside of California, the struggle is far from over. We will continue the struggle in states without marriage equality until it's achieved, with a great advantage. The example of California and the twelve other states with marriage equality will be enormous. The contrast of those states where all marriages enjoy all the federal and state rights and benefits will be stark. Pressure will mount as one state, then another, grants marriage equality. It will be hard to maintain old prejudices and the rigid confines of traditional marriage over time. People will see there really is no good reason to object any longer.

The worst case is for both DOMA and Prop 8 to be upheld. There is only one recourse now: a federal amendment to the U.S. Constitution. As more and more states grant marriage equality, it will be easier to pass a federal amendment which requires a 2/3 majority, or 34 states. With the majority of Americans now supporting same-sex marriage, and rapidly growing, it will be hard to stop such an effort. Federal amendments are proposed in Congress but ratified in state legislatures which are much closer to the people and therefore more inclined to do their will. So there is hope, with justification, that even this case is not the end of the struggle; not even close.

We're not likely to get a sweeping victory, but there is a way ahead, nevertheless. The worst thing we can do is give up. As Martin Luther King Jr. said, "The arc of the moral universe is long but it bends toward justice." The arc has brought us an end to slavery, segregation, and apartheid, the emancipation of women, and the beginning of universal gay rights. The next great breakthrough is just ahead.

Chapter 9 Discussion Starters

1. Now that the Supreme Court has decided, how do you feel about the decisions?

2. What ideas do you have for continuing to work for gay rights?

3. What remains to be accomplished to gain full LGBT equality?

4. Why do government officials swear on the Bible to uphold the Constitution and not swear on the Constitution to uphold the Bible?

5. What are your thoughts about the popular vote versus the Constitution? Which should decide?

10

How to Get Involved

How wonderful it is that nobody need wait
a single moment before starting to improve the
world. ~ Anne Frank

What You Can Do to Support Same-sex Marriage

You can make a difference! Everyone has a sphere of influence, whether it is just your family, Facebook friends, a congregation, or much broader. These are people who look to you to help them form opinions. They don't expect you to do their thinking for them, but they do appreciate hearing your views.

1. The first thing you can do is express your sincerely held opinions. You may be surprised at how open people are to discuss this now that it is in the realm of respectable conversation. This will give you an opportunity to bring solid information to bear on the subject, that is, if you know what you're talking about. Unsupported opinions are easily dismissed as mere prejudicial thinking.

2. Be sure that you know what you're talking about. There are a variety of ways to increase your knowledge of this subject and you don't even have to leave your iPad. Just Google "same-sex marriage" and a world of information is open to you online or in your local library. Some of my favorites include: www.soulforce,org; http://en.wikipedia.org/wiki/Status_of_samesex_marriage. See also http://

www.thetaskforce.org/; http://www.aclu.org/lgbt-rights/
lgbt-relationships; http://www.prop8trialtracker.com/
These will get you started and will lead you even deeper
into the subject.

3. If you feel confident of your ability to persuade, get yourself
    invited to speak or to lead discussions in service organizations,
    churches, schools, and town gatherings. Start out in your own
    living room, if necessary. This is a leading topic and people
    are eager for solid information.

4. Write an opinion column for your local newspaper, or letters
    to the editor.

5. Sign up for the Human Rights Campaign's "Millions for
    Marriage."
    http://www.hrc.org/millions-for-marriage#.
    UOUEwm9X3HQ There is a lot of additional information
    available on this site as well.

6. Find out the positions of your political representatives and
    lobby them for support. If they aren't helpful, work for those
    who are. VOTE and encourage others, as well.

7. Be supportive of your gay friends and family. They are often
    left alone and appreciate a caring heart. If you are straight,
    nothing is more persuasive than an ally in the struggle.

8. If you have some extra cash, donate to organizations that
    support this mission. Also, donate your time and talents. We
    are always working on a shoestring and stretched beyond our
    means.

9. Get acquainted with your local LGBT Center. Find one
    close to you here:
    http://www.lgbtcenters.org/Centers/find-a center.aspx

This list is surely partial; there is much more we can do.

Email me at info@clergyunited.org and let me know what you
are involved in, and if there is any way I can help you, I will. Doing
something, no matter how much or little, makes a difference. You
can make a difference!

What you can say to your friends about same-sex marriage

Same-sex marriage is becoming less and less controversial as more states (and nations) are legalizing it, while books and articles on all sides of the issue abound. It is a topic that has come of age. Likely, you have been involved in discussions about this. If you are unclear about how to think about same-sex marriage, or about how best to frame your responses, these suggestions may help.

"Marriage has always been between one man and one woman."

This is almost too easy to refute. I am puzzled how anyone can hold this view. The cynical side of me thinks that no educated person really believes this. So, remind people that Abraham, King David, Solomon, and a host of Old Testament patriarchs had many wives and polygamy was tolerated under the Law of Moses. In the New Testament, Paul advises that an Elder (congregational leader) should have only one wife, suggesting that polygamy was still in use among some Christians.

And to make matters worse for those who would make marriage between one man and one woman the ideal, both Paul and Jesus forswear marriage for Christians if at all possible. The ideal is a celibate life; marriage is considered an encumbrance to spreading the gospel.

"Since the Bible condemns homosexuality, giving it the cover of marriage does not change the fact that it is a sin."

In the first place, America is not a theocracy. Our Constitution governs us, not the Bible. So the mere fact that the Bible condemns anything is irrelevant. Do we make gluttony or pride unlawful just because the Bible says they are sins? Of course not.

"If we allow gay marriage, what's next? Polygamy? Child brides? Where will it end, marrying our pets?"

This is commonly known as the "slippery slope" argument. The fact that any supposed next step may be undesirable is irrelevant. What is at issue is the worthwhileness of same-sex marriage. It should stand or fall on its own merits, not on what may or may not ensue. Opponents of the ban on assault weapons in 1994 claimed that the next step would be the banning of all rifles and eventually the confiscation of all guns. The next step was actually the repeal of the ban on assault weapons. The government's argument for sending troops to Vietnam was called the "domino effect." If we let Vietnam fall, then its neighbors will fall and we will lose the entire of South East Asia to the communists. Vietnam fell to the communists. No other nations fell. Today, we have normalized relations and Vietnam is a member of the UN, the World Trade Organization and a threat to no one.

The slippery slope argument is resorted to when good arguments are no longer available. By using this, opponents of same-sex marriage are admitting they have nothing of value left to say.

"Marriage is only for the purpose of procreation. LGBTs can't procreate, so they aren't eligible for marriage."

This is another of those arguments that stretch credibility. This argument is made by the Roman Catholic Church and other religious groups, but even they don't honor it, for they will marry people well beyond the age to procreate, and those who are of child-bearing age but can't conceive.

Only the most wooden literalists would insist on limiting the definition of procreation to "sperm meets egg." Procreation, that is, creating a family, is not only possible among LGBTs but happening every day. Adoption is one of the most urgent needs today. Gay families have proven themselves to be appropriate options for raising a family. Same-sex marriage would aid in making this possible.

"Legalizing same-sex marriage will harm traditional marriages."

The easiest way to defuse this objection is to ask a simple question: Tell me just how your marriage will be harmed? In asking this countless times, I have yet to get any answer at all. Not just a poor answer, but no answer.

To broaden the issue just a bit, if it is suggested that legalizing same-sex marriage will impact traditional families, they are correct. Their children will be obliged to recognize that some of their playmates have two mommies or daddies. This will certainly raise questions for their moms and dads. Schools will likely have to deal with same-sex relations in health classes. However, both situations already exist. Not legalizing same-sex marriage won't change this. Recognizing it will mean that we will have open discussions and fact- based research, such as the realization that gayness isn't an airborne disease that we catch by being in the same room with it. The children of opposite-sex parents won't more easily become gay by association; their parents have nothing to fear. If their children turn out to be gay, it is for other reasons altogether.

"Okay, then, you tell me why same-sex marriage is a good thing!"

Same-sex couples face the same challenges and problems that opposite-sex couples who are married face, yet are without the same resources to meet these challenges. There are an estimated 1,139 federal benefits presently withheld from them as well as many state benefits. America is all about equal rights. LGBTs couples that are unable to marry are being discrimin-ated against.

What to say to your friends about the Bible and Homosexuality

So often we're in situations where someone says something that puts down a family member or a friend, but we're not sure how to go about dealing with it. Here are some suggested replies that must be said with a smile on your face and love in your heart.

The response of consistency

"**Although** you may believe that the Bible condemns homosexuals, it also condemns many things which we accept today. These include eating pork, growing hybrid crops, working on Saturday, and women wearing pants. How can it be proper to cling to this one prohibition and dismiss the others?"

Explanation: Most people want to be consistent, or are a little embarrassed when an inconsistency is pointed out. The burden is now on them to try to explain how this case is an exception. They will fail.

The response of more light

"**The** Bible also approves of many things we condemn today, including polygamy, slavery, levirate marriage, subordination of women, and genocide. Your disapproval of these things (that the Bible approves) indicates that you don't believe that just because the Bible once considered them proper that they are necessarily right for us today. Surely you don't continue to believe in these things?"

Explanation: We learn more and we move ahead.

The response of proper motivation

"I've looked at the Bible verses that seem to condemn homosexuality. Most of them have nothing to do with homosexuality. The most that can be said is that certain same-sex acts were condemned because the people were turning sex into an idol and acting out of lust. All opposite-sex acts stemming from the same reasons were condemned also. It isn't the kind of sex that's wrong, just the motivations for doing it."

Explanation: Forcing a wife to have sex is rape; only if mutually agreed to is sex proper, even between married couples. Things are often right or wrong depending upon the reasons for doing them.

The response of logic

"Did you know there is no word in Hebrew or Greek (the languages of the Bible) for homosexual? How can the Bible be said to condemn what it doesn't know exists?"

Explanation: The word homosexual was coined in the 19th century. The word sodomy (Latin, sodomia) was coined 1000 years after the Bible was written. Semanticists tell us that if there is no word, there is no idea behind it.

The response of love

"I'm not a scholar, so I can't say I have studied the issues completely, but I can say that what Jesus expects from us is very simple: We are to love one another. What we must be about is removing the barriers between people, not helping to maintain them in their rigid place."

Explanation: It's the Golden Rule. By the way, the Golden Rule is PROactive in that we are to DO to others, not merely NOT DOING the bad.

The response of Pro-life

"When Jesus' disciples violated the Sabbath by feeding themselves, he taught us that laws are to serve humans, not stand in their way. Even the Sabbath law, the violation of which meant being stoned to death, could be set aside for the sake of human compassion. Jesus would say that laws or beliefs that serve to dehumanize anyone, including homosexuals, need to be discarded."

Explanation: There is no higher morality than upholding the dignity of a human. Any religious notion that tells you it is OK to denigrate, dehumanize or otherwise withhold good to another is wrong on the face of it. It is actually evil to do so.

Chapter 10 Discussion Starters

1. Do you believe you can make a difference? How?

2. What do you plan to do, specifically?

3. What is needed for your congregation to understand the issues better?

4. Which of the "What to Say..." items will be helpful to you? Which need more explanation?

5. Have you seen the documentary, "For the Bible Tells Me So"? If so, what can you share about it?

6. How have your views changed, if they have changed, since reading this book?

A Word to Pastors

When Welcoming Is More Than Toleration

As pastors, we are well aware of the courage it takes for many first-time visitors to find their way into our sanctuaries. They often have to deal with poor signage, lack of a welcoming face, and even hostility over where they choose to sit. In many ways visitors are as much a threat to a congregation as promise.

Imagine then what it takes for a gay person to show up for worship. All the above is compounded by a real or perceived sense of animosity toward who they are, even if it is not obvious at first sight. After all, the church's reputation in the gay community as a hostile environment for them is well deserved.

I often attend PFLAG (Parents and Friends of Lesbians and Gays) meetings, and have spoken on occasion. My congregation was officially "Open and Affirming," and I was well known as a gay advocate in the community. After a period of many months and a lot of exposure, gays began to see that even though I was straight, I was for real. Surely, I thought, some of them will attend my church, and when they do, they will find a warm and affirming welcome. Several years of regular contact went by and not a single gay person came to worship with us. So, I shared my frustration with a gay friend who knew the situation well. His response hit me like an arrow through the heart. "Oh, they trust you alright, but because of

their horrific experiences in their own churches, they are unwilling
to trust strangers, no matter how sincerely they are approached."

Ever since then, it has been my continual pursuit to find out
how congregations can grow into a truly welcoming body that
will not only attract gay visitors, but will allow themselves to be
nourished by them, as well. Until congregations discover the joy
of integrating gays into their communities, they will continue to,
as they say, "stay away in droves."

Of course, not all pastors are committed to being open and
affirming of gays, lesbians, bisexuals and transgenders (LGBTs).
Yet, many of you want to be at least welcoming, and consider
yourself and your congregation open if not affirming. Please read
on, as you may discover that you and/or your congregation may
not be as open as you think.

Here are several questions I'm often asked:
*As pastors committed to ministry to all who come our way, what
do you see as your role in the life of a LGBT person? How can you be
the most help? What is the most important thing you could do to offer
pastoral care and support?*

I'll start with the last question first, as it will form the basis for
the remaining answers.

Contrary to the conventional wisdom held by most pastors,
what gays, lesbians, bisexuals and transgender people desire most
from a congregation is not affirmation or acceptance; what they
want (and deserve) is to worship in safety. I define safety as a
congregational culture devoid of spiritual violence. Affirmation
and acceptance will accompany safety, but as long as there is the
possibility of spiritual violence breaking out (except accidentally),
LGBTs will not take a congregation, or its pastor, seriously.

What is spiritual violence? It is the condemnation and sus-
tained abuse heaped upon LGBT people in the name of Jesus
Christ.

One summer not too long ago, I received a call from a congregant who said that a relative was visiting and wanted to attend our church so he could let us have it over our affirming stance. He planned on interrupting our worship service where he would point out our sinful ways.

Naturally, this caused quite a bit of anxiety for me, as I have witnessed such outbursts before, but never during worship. However, I soon found that the congregation leaders were not in the least upset. They saw this as a means to demonstrate their solidarity with their gay members. So we devised a plan that we would implement if our hostile visitor's words began to be abusive. The choir and musicians were prompted, at my signal, to rise and begin singing "They Will Know We Are Christians by Our Love." The leaders in the audience would also stand and sing, urging others to join in. In no time, the visitor would be drowned out and his relative would suggest they leave. As long as he stayed put, we would sing. If further coaxing would not work, the police would be called.

The relative decided to stay home. We were not able to provide what would have been a powerful witness.

My point is this: we will not be able to avoid all forms of spiritual abuse of our gay members and visitors, but we can have plans in place that ensure continued safety.

Consequently, a pastor's most important role is to foster a safe congregational environment. This is accomplished initially by personal example. Modeling of acceptance, affirmation, and not allowing spiritual violence to go unchallenged are critical. Then, promoting qualified LGBTs to leadership positions is vital. If the pastor's demeanor toward LGBTs is a part of a comprehensive undertaking regarding all oppressed peoples, this will avoid LGBTs as being perceived as pastor's pets, and will be more easily accepted by the congregation.

Another caution is not to treat LGBTs only as objects of concern and ministry. This creates an imbalance between straights and gays and is a reflection of heterosexism. In other words, straights may think of LGBTs as "unfortunately that way", and wish they were straight ("for their own good"). This is translated into "straight is better" and is a form of spiritual violence.

What is needed is to use gayness as a model for human/Christian betterment. I highly recommend L. William Countryman and M. R. Ritley's, *Gifted by Otherness*, as a good introduction to God's gift to the church that is gayness. Here's a quote, p. 151.

> "It is our [LGBTs] very woundedness, the fractures that we carry as a separate people in a hostile and condemning world that makes us pervious to God's spirit, open to the shattering and healing life of God in Christ. Life has not given us security enough to rest in the cocoon of custom or inherited beliefs: we are more vulnerable, both to the worst the world can do to us and to the best that God can cause to happen in us. In a sense, we are the doorways through which God can enter a society, a church grown deaf to God's good news."

Now THAT is a gift!!! The problem straight Christians have is our imperviousness to God's spirit based on our power and privileged position in church and society. By way of example, the only difference between 12 step alcoholics and the rest of us is that they deeply understand their total dependence on God in ways the non-alcoholic is reluctant to acknowledge. Yes, LGBTs have much to teach us. (See Chapter 8, "The Gifts Gays Bring.)

As a pastor of an "Open and Affirming" congregation, I peppered my personal and public remarks with such things as, "As an open and affirming church, we…", and, "As a people committed to overcoming injustice, we…", and, "As a congregation which stands with the oppressed, we…." I never, ever let up on these self-affirmations, as we need constant reminders of who we are, and we are never fully what we want to be. It's important to remind ourselves that even open and affirming churches begin as open and hope to become affirming. Taking an open church to an affirming church is one of the great joys of pastoral leadership. Taking a closed church to open is grounds for sainthood.

If your heart is not committed to overcoming the church's failure to receive our gay brothers and sisters with affirmation and integrity, don't bother; your true attitude will soon (if not imme-diately) surface and you will be just another reason why they won't come to our churches.

Perhaps another caveat is in order. When naming hetero-sexism as the virulent sin that it is, be sure to model the axiom to "love the sinner while hating the sin." After all, God loves everyone, including heterosexists.

AFTERWORD

Some men see things as they are and say "why." I
dream things that never were and say "why not."
~ Robert F. Kennedy

Just as I was about to sit at my computer to begin writing this afterword, I checked the incoming news. And what did I find? Uruguay just made same-sex unions equal to opposite-sex unions. Uruguay! It's joining Argentina, Portugal, and Spain, three other predominantly Roman Catholic nations (with France not far behind) in the process, along with eleven other nations. I didn't know whether to whoop or weep what with the reluctance here in America. If solidly Roman Catholic nations can see their way into the emancipation of their LGBT citizens, America cannot be far behind. In the words of Sir Winston Churchill, "You can always count on Americans to do the right thing—after they've tried everything else."

First, a word to my lesbian, gay, bisexual, and transgender friends. For many of you, your experience in the heterosexist world has been uncomfortable, if not downright abusive. Much of that negativity comes from Christian sources, but not all. If you are a member of a Christian church, you are to be commended for your tenacity. I thank God that you are there; that you are witnessing to the power of the gospel to make one whole in spite of a world that seeks to render you impotent. We need you there. We need your gifts, your voice, your witness. Without you, we will never be the church we can be. With you, no one, regardless of their circumstances, ever needs to feel outside the love of God.

If you are not a member of a church, or even a Christian, because of the way Christians have treated you, know that there are many thousands of us, even millions, who would welcome you. For far too long the Christian Right has controlled the message to such an extent that all Christians are marred by their hurtful rhetoric and are assumed to speak with only one voice. But the tide is turning. The Christian Church (Disciples of Christ), the United Church of Christ, the Evangelical Lutheran Church in America, and The Society of Friends (Quakers), have many welcoming churches, along with the Unitarians and Unity Churches.

And to my straight allies, you are to be commended for standing with the oppressed in spite of often difficult times. Nothing is more important to those who are working to engage the forces arrayed against oppression than for people of good will to stand with them in the trenches. Sometimes this has and will mean sacrificing your time, talent, money, and even your reputations for the sake of the cause. No matter. When the disciples complained to Jesus that they had left everything to follow him, he replied that whatever is lost is made up for in the company of the committed. You know this is true, for just as with the Psalmist, you have "tasted and seen that it is good."

A Select Bibliography
of Resources

What Is Homosexuality?

Calhoun, John B. "Population Density and Social Pathology." *Scientific American* 206:139-148, 1962.
  Definitive study of effects of overpopulation that produces homosexuality in animals.

Greenberg, David. *The Construction of Homosexuality.* The University of Chicago Press, 1988.

Minor, Robert N. *Scared Straight: Why It's So Hard to Accept Gay people and Why It's so Hard to Be Human.* Humanity Works!, 2001.
  A thorough-going constructionist approach to gender issues. Clearly shows how gender and sexual roles are created and reinforced and why deviance is punished. Offers a way out of heterosexism into healthy sexuality for everyone. The definitive work attempting to show that homosexuality is socially constructed as opposed to essentialist (born that way). Scholarly, yet accessible.

Mondimore, Francis Mark. *A Natural History of Homosexuality.* The Johns Hopkins University Press, 1996.

Essential! Provides a comprehensive yet highly accessible overview of all aspects of current scholarship on homosexuality (except biblical). Eminently readable. This book is a must have, but you will have to get lucky with a used book seller.

Interpreting the Bible

Borg, Marcus J. *Reading the Bible Again for the First Time: Taking the Bible Seriously But Not Literally.* HarperCollins, 2001.

An easy, yet powerful introduction to biblical interpretation that takes modern science, other faith traditions and biblical critiques seriously. Helps the reader understand how to separate the words of the Bible from the Word of God.

Boswell, John. *Christianity, Social Tolerance, and Homosexuality: Gay People in Western Europe from the Beginning of the Christian Era to the Fourteenth Century.* The University of Chicago Press, 1981.

Easily the most extensive and comprehensive study of the questions central to Christianity and homosexuality. His work in exegeting scripture is groundbreaking. Everybody must deal with Boswell, and he's not easily contradicted. Although he is considered an essentialist, he is sympathetic to the social constructionists.

Brawley, Robert. L., Editor. *Biblical Ethics and Homosexuality: Listening to Scripture.* Westminster John Knox Press, 1996.

Noted biblical scholars deal with such issues in the sexuality debate as how to make ancient scripture accessible to modern readers, what scriptures to listen to and not to listen to, background information on the ancient Near East, and not all are written from the same point of view. Fills in many of the holes left by others.

Countryman, L. William. *Dirt, Greed and Sex: Sexual Ethics in the New Testament and Their Implications for Today.* Fortress Press, 1988.

Perhaps the finest exegesis of biblical passages relevant to homosexuality. Although it is often heavy going, the payoff is well worth the effort. He presents a convincing case that Romans 1 has nothing to do with sin, along with a couple of h u n d r e d other compelling observations.

Furnish, Victor Paul. *The Moral Teachings of Paul.* Abingdon Press, 1985.
Provides good background material that sets the New Testament "clobber passages" in their social settings. Undermines the common mistranslations and misinterpretations that lead to homophobic reading of the Bible.

Helminiak, Daniel A. *What the Bible Really Says about Homosexuality (Millennium Edition).* Alamo Square Press, 2000.
This is the book to begin with since Mondimore did not cover the biblical material. He explains in clear and readable fashion the scholarly research on the so-called "clobber passages" of the Bible. Very useful as a refresher to the "Beyond the Bible and Homosexuality"seminar.

Jordan, Mark D. *The Invention of Sodomy in Christian Theology.* University of Chicago, 1997.
A scholarly investigation that explores the historical development of the sin of sodomy. Traces how the church in the Middle Ages invented a sin that did not exist prior to its invention, and shows its long-standing effects on same-sex relationships. This is not easy reading, but very rewarding.

Nissinen, Marti. *Homoeroticism in the Biblical World.* Fortress Press, 1998
Surveys the ancient Near Eastern literature contemporaneous with the Bible and sheds light on how to understand biblical concepts of sexuality. Demonstrates the erroneous procedure of confusing biblical and ancient concepts of sexuality with modern concepts.

Scroggs, Robin. *The New Testament and Homosexuality.* Fortress Press, 1983.

A core volume that treats all the relevant New Testament texts in a scholarly but readable fashion. Some say it's the best resource of its kind.

Biblical Theology

Alexander, Marilyn Bennett and James Preston. *We Were Baptized Too: Claiming God's Grace for Lesbians and Gays.* Westminster John Knox Press, 1996.

Challenges the church to take seriously its understanding of baptism and communion as means of grace, justice, and liberation. Charges the church with abandoning gays and lesbians who they baptized with the promise to accept, love, forgive and nurture, and calls the church to repentance.

Countryman, L. William and M. R. Ritley. *Gifted by Otherness: Gay and Lesbian Christians in the Church.* Moorehouse Publishing, 2001.

This proactive and self-affirming book provides new hope for the LGBT community, their families, and their communities, confidently appropriating and retelling the biblical story of this unique and gifted minority's spiritual journey. In short, it's about being gay and Christian from the inside while not repudiating the larger church.

Johnson, William Stacy. *A Time to Embrace: Same-Gender Relationships in Religion, Law, and Politics.* William B. Eerdmans Publishing, 2006

Straight lawyer-theologian ties gay affirmation to biblical theology by using the categories of creation, reconciliation in Christ, and redemption. Also offers excellent reasons for gay marriage. My choice for those who want only one book.

McNeill, John J. *Taking a Chance on God.* Beacon Press, 1996.

A former Roman Catholic priest speaks directly to gay and lesbian Christians about why it makes sense not to abandon the faith. His writings reflect the anguish and despair many gays and lesbians feel and offers life-giving options that all can embrace and be made whole.

Scanzoni, Letha Dawson and Virginia Ramey Mollenkott. *Is the Homosexual My Neighbor? A Positive Response.* Harper & Row, 1994.

Groundbreaking work in 1978 that looks at homosexuality from scientific, psychological, and biblical perspectives. Completely revised in 1994. A wide-ranging synthesis of a lot of material found throughout this bibliography. A good choice for reading only one book.

Homophobia and Its Consequences

Blumenfeld, Warren J. *Homophobia: How We All Pay the Price.* Beacon Press, 1992.

Points out the hidden costs of homophobia in family relationships, religious institutions, social policy, and many other aspects of our lives. Offers concrete suggestions for transforming attitudes, behaviors, and institutions.

Fone, Byrne. *Homophobia: A History.* Metropolitan Books, 2000.

Chronicles the evolution of homophobia through the centuries. Deals well with biblical texts, particularly on Sodom and Gomorrah. Especially good at describing the sexual understandings of antiquity.

Jung, Patricia Beattie and Ralph F. Smith. *Heterosexism: An Ethical Challenge.* State University of New York Press, 1993

Takes apart the sociological underpinnings of heterosexism and exposes their harmful effects on us all. Particularly good at helping gays and straights alike see how we are all imprisoned in certain false assumptions about reality that we need to be freed from in order to be truly human. Particularly useful in helping the church to understand the larger issues and offers a way to reform the church and society.

Gay Life in America

Bawer, Bruce. *A Place at the Table: The Gay Individual in American Society.* Touchstone, 1993.

    Refutes the arguments used by antigay activists to stir groundless fears and hostility, and also offers a frank critique of an unrepresentative gay subculture that falsely equates homosexuality with promiscuity, hedonism, and political correctness. A great book to share with your friends who believe homosexuality is only sex, sex, and more sex.

White, Mell. *Stranger at the Gate: To Be Gay and Christian in America.* Simon and Schuster, 1994.

    The founder of Soulforce and former ghost writer for Jerry Falwell, Pat Roberston and Billy Graham, shares his struggle to be gay and Christian. The single best first-person look at how a God-fearing man tried every conceivable means to rid himself of his "abominating affliction" only to discover that God loves and accepts him just as he is. More than any other book, this one is convincing evidence that the center of the homosexual life is truly no different than that of the heterosexual.

History of the Gay Rights Movement

Clendinen, Dudley and Adam Nagourney. *Out for Good: The Struggle to Build a Gay Rights Movement in America.* Simon and Schuster, 1999.

    The best single volume history of the gay rights struggle in America. It answers some nagging questions such as why the movement is so diverse politically, why gays and lesbians originally couldn't get along, and why the movement can't settle on a unified vision.

In Defense of the Traditional Interpretations

Balch, David L., Editor. *Homosexuality, Science, and the APlain Sense@ of Scripture.* William B. Eerdmnas Publishing Company, 2000.

Ten scholars, progressive and conservative square off in debating the issues. Gives a good overview of the different ways of doing biblical interpretation.

Gagnon, Robert A. J. *The Bible and Homosexual Practice.* Abingdon Press, 2001.

The most current scholarly defense of the traditional understanding of homosexuality and the Bible. Ironically, given the title, he relies more on "Natural Law" than the Bible. Most traditionalists view this as the best defense to date.

Hays, Richard B. *The Moral Vision of the New Testament.* Harper-SanFrancisco, 1996.

Chapter 16, on Homosexuality, offers a highly nuanced interpretation of the relevant passages in the New Testament. Some consider this superior to Gagnon's.

Schmidt, Thomas E. *Straight & Narrow?* InterVarsity Press, 1995.

Attempts to answer the arguments for acceptance of homosexuals. Offers scriptural exegesis, deals with whether or not people are born with homosexual orientations, and takes on John Boswell. Wants to "hate the sin but love the sinner". Fails.

Reparative Therapy

Besen, Wayne R. *Anything But Straight: Unmasking the Scandals and Lies Behind the Ex-Gay Myth.* Harrington Park Press, 2003

An expose' of the ex-gay and reparative therapy movements from the inside. Shows the connections between them and the radical right, and the damage they do.

Bibles

Peterson, Eugene H. *The Message: The Bible in Contemporary Language.* NavPress, 2002.

This is the only Bible that even comes close to dealing with the "clobber passages" with integrity.

Michael Coogan, Editor. T*he New Oxford Annotated Bible.* Third Edition. Oxford University Press, 2001.

Its scholarly notes reflect current research, and is fair in its treatment of the relevant passages.

Index of Subjects

ALPHABETICAL INDEX
OF SCRIPTURES

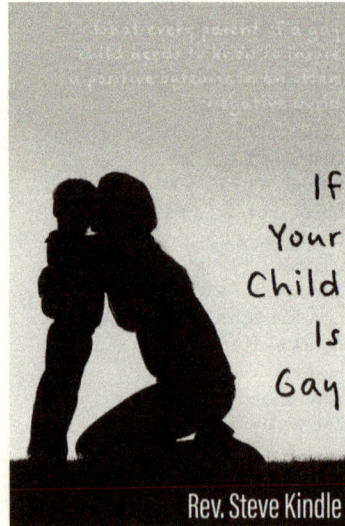

MORE FROM ENERGION PUBLICATIONS

Personal Study

Finding God in Suffering	Bruce G. Epperly	$9.99
The Jesus Paradigm	David Alan Black	$17.99
When People Speak for God	Henry Neufeld	$17.99
The Sacred Journey	Chris Surber	$11.99

Christian Living

Faith in the Public Square	Robert D. Cornwall	$16.99
Grief: Finding the Candle of Light	Jody Neufeld	$8.99
Crossing the Street	Robert LaRochelle	$16.99

Bible Study

Learning and Living Scripture	Lentz/Neufeld	$12.99
From Inspiration to Understanding	Edward W. H. Vick	$24.99
Galatians: A Participatory Study Guide	Bruce G. Epperly	$12.99
Philippians: A Participatory Study Guide	Bruce Epperly	$9.99
Ephesians: A Participatory Study Guide	Robert D. Cornwall	$9.99

Theology

Creation in Scripture	Herold Weiss	$12.99
Creation: the Christian Doctrine	Edward W. H. Vick	$12.99
The Politics of Witness	Allan R. Bevere	$9.99
Ultimate Allegiance	Robert D. Cornwall	$9.99
History and Christian Faith	Edward W. H. Vick	$9.99
The Church Under the Cross	William Powell Tuck	$11.99
The Journey to the Undiscovered Country	William Powell Tuck	$9.99
Eschatology: A Participatory Study Guide	Edward W. H. Vick	$9.99

Ministry

Clergy Table Talk	Kent Ira Groff	$9.99
Out of the Office	Robert D. Cornwall	$9.99

Generous Quantity Discounts Available
Dealer Inquiries Welcome
Energion Publications — P.O. Box 841
Gonzalez, FL_ 32560
Website: http://energionpubs.com
Phone: (850) 525-3916